孫子兵法

II

# Sun Tzu's
# *Art of War*
# Playbook
## Volume 2 of 9:
# Perspective

Gary Gagliardi

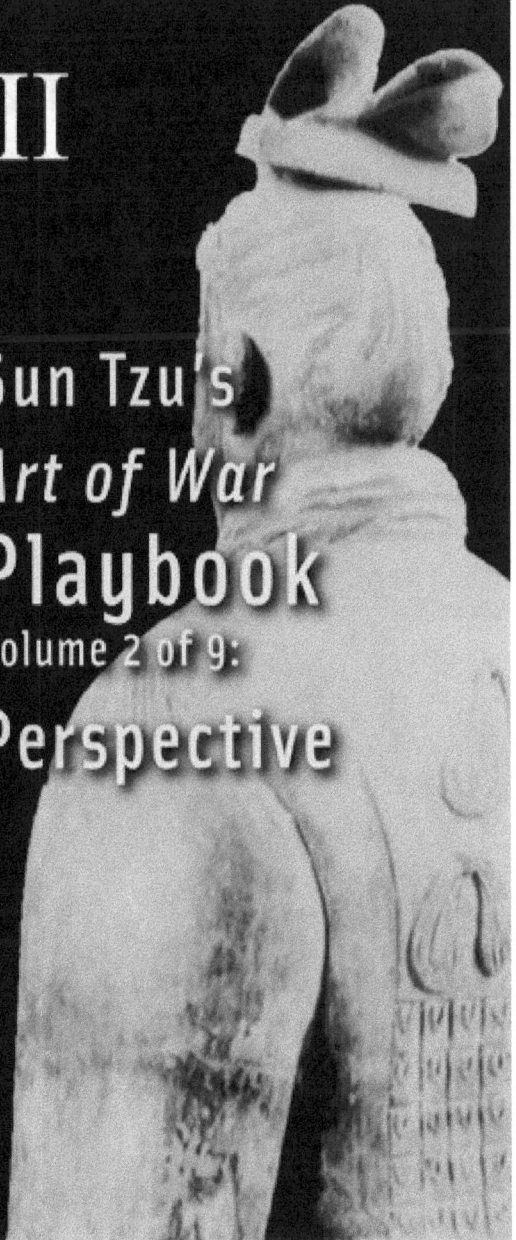

# Sun Tzu's Art of War Playbook

## Volume Two: Perspective

by Gary Gagliardi
The Science of Strategy Institute
Clearbridge Publishing

Published by
Science of Strategy Institute, Clearbridge Publishing
 suntzus.com     scienceofstrategy.org

First Print Edition
Library of Congress Control Number: 2014909969
Also sold as an ebook under the title Sun Tzu's Warrior Rule Book
Copyright 2010, 2011, 2012, 2013, 2014 Gary Gagliardi
ISBN 978-1-929194-77-3 (13-digit) 1-929194-77-3 (10-digit)

Originally published as a series of articles on the Science of Strategy Website, scienceofstratregy.org. and
later as an ebook on various sites.

PO Box 33772, Seattle, WA 98133
Phone: (206)542-8947 Fax: (206)546-9756
beckyw@clearbridge.com
garyg@scienceofstrategy.org

Manufactured in the United States of America.
Interior and cover graphic design by Dana and Jeff Wincapaw.
Original Chinese calligraphy by Tsai Yung, Green Dragon Arts, www.greendragonarts.com.

Publisher's Cataloging-in-Publication Data
Sun-tzu, 6th cent. B.C.
Strategy
    [Sun-tzu ping fa, English]
    Art of War Playbook / Sun Tzu and Gary Gagliardi.
    p.197  cm. 23
    Includes introduction to basic competitive philosophy of Sun Tzu

Clearbridge Publishing's books may be purchased for business, for any promotional use,
or for special sales.

# Contents

# Playbook Overview

*Note: This overview is provided for those who have not read the previous volume of* Sun Tzu's Art of War Playbook. *It provides an brief overview of the work in general and the general concepts framing the first volume.*

Sun Tzu's **The Art of War** is less a "book" in the modern Western sense than it is an outline for a course of study. Like Euclid's Geometry, simply reading the work teaches us very little. Sun Tzu wrote in in a tradition that expected each line and stanza to be studied in the context of previous statements to build up the foundation for understanding later statements.

To make this work easier for today's readers to understand, we developed the **Strategy Playbook**, the Science of Strategy Institute (SOSI) guidebook to explaining Sun Tzu's strategy in the more familiar format of a series of explanations with examples. These lessons are framed in the context of modern competition rather than ancient military warfare.

This Playbook is the culmination of over a decade of work breaking down Sun Tzu's principles into a series of step-by-step practical articles by the Institute's multiple award-winning author and founder, Gary Gagliardi. The original **Art of War** was written for military generals who understood the philosophical concepts of ancient China, which in itself is a practical hurdle that most modern readers cannot clear. Our Art of War Playbook is written for today's reader. It puts Sun Tzu's ideas into everyday, practical language.

The Playbook defines a new science of strategic competition aimed at today's challenges. This science of competition is designed as the complementary opposite of the management science that is taught in most business schools. This science starts, as Sun Tzu did himself, by defining a better, more complete vocabulary for discussing competitive situations. It connects the timeless ideas of Sun Tzu to today's latest thinking in business, mathematics, and psychology.

The entire Playbook consists of two hundred and thirty articles describing over two-thousand interconnected key methods. These articles are organized into nine different areas of strategic skill from understanding positioning to defending vulnerabilities. All together this makes up over a thousand pages of material.

## Playbook Access

The Playbook's most up-to-date version is available as separate articles on our website. Live links make it easy to access the connections between various articles and concepts. If you become a SOSI Member, you can access any Playbook article at any time and access their links.

However, at the request of our customers, we also offer these articles as a series of nine eBooks. Each of the nine sections of the entire Playbook makes up a separate eBook, Playbook Parts One Through Nine. These parts flow logically through the Progress Cycle of listen-aim-move-claim (see illustration). Because of the dynamic nature of the on-line version, these eBooks are not going to be as current as the on-line version. You can see a outline of current Playbook articles here and, generally, the eBook version will contain most of the same material in the same order.

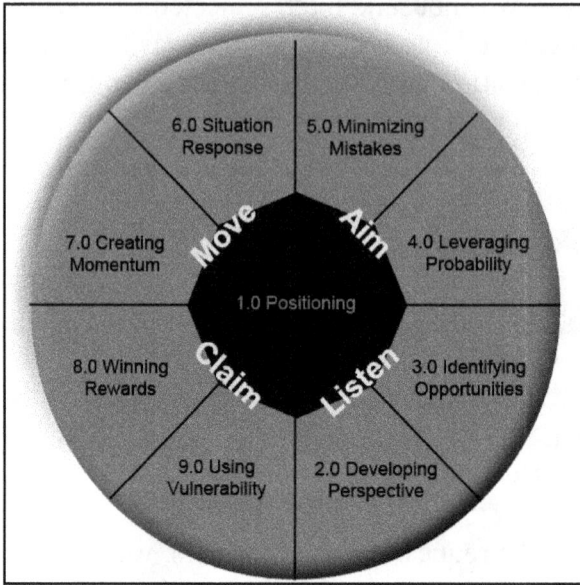

Nine categories of strategic skills define cycle that advances our positions:

1. Comparing Positions,

2. Developing Perspective,

3. Identifying Opportunities,

4. Leveraging Probability,

5. Minimizing Mistakes,

6. Responding To Situations,

7. Creating Momentum,

8. Winning Rewards, And

9. Defending Vulnerabilities.

## Playbook Structure and Design

These articles are written in **standard format** including 1) the general principle, 2) the situation, 3) the opportunity, 4) the list of specific Art of War key methods breaking down the general principle into a series of actions, and 5) an illustration of the application of each of those key methods to a specific competitive situation. Key methods are written generically to apply to every competitive arena (business, personal life, career, sports, relationships, etc.) with each specific illustrations drawn from one of these areas.

A number identifies where each article appears in Playbook Structure. For example, the article <u>2.1.3 Strategic Deception</u> is the third article in the first section of the second book in the nine volumes of the Strategy Playbook. In our on-line version, these links are live, clicking on them brings you to the article itself. We provide them because the interconnection of concepts is important in learning Sun Tzu's system.

## Playbook Training

Training in Sun Tzu's **warrior skills** does not entail memorizing all these principles. Instead, these concepts are used to develop exercises and tools that allow trainees to put this ideas in practice. While each rule is useful, the heart of Sun Tzu system is the methods that connect all the principles together. Training in these principles is designed to develop a **gut instinct** for how Sun Tzu's strategy is used in different situations to produce success. Principles are interlinked because they describe a comprehensive conceptual **mental model**. Warrior Class training puts trainees in a situation where they must constantly make decisions, rewarding them for making decisions consist with **winning productively instead of destructively**.

# About Positions

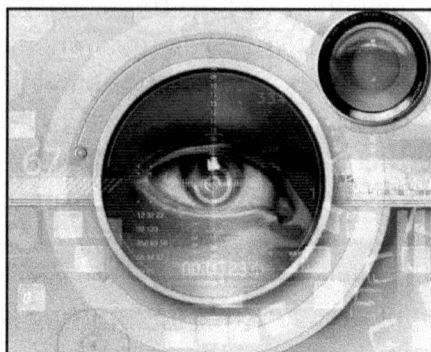

This first volume of Sun Tzu's Playbook focuses on teaching us the nature of strategic positions. "Position awareness" gives you a framework for understanding your strategic situation relative to the conditions around you. It enables you to see your position as part of a larger environment constructed of other positions and the raw elements that create positions. Master Sun Tzu's system of comparing positions, you can understand which aspect of your position are secure and which are the most dynamic and likely to change.

Traditional strategy defines a "position" as a comparison of situations. Game theory defines is as the current decision point that is arrive at as the sum or result of all previous decisions, both yours and those of others. Sun Tzu's methods of positioning awareness are different. They force you to see yourself in the eyes of others. Using these techniques, you broaden your perspective by gathering a range of viewpoints. In a limited sense, the scope of your position defines your area of control within your larger environment. In traditional strategy, five elements--mission, climate, ground, command, and methods--define the dimensions in which competitors can be compared.

## Competition as Comparison

Sun Tzu saw that success is based on comparisons. This comparison must take place whenever a choice is made. For Sun Tzu, competition means a comparison of alternative choices or "positions". Battles are won by positioning before they are fought. These positions provide choices for everyone involved. Good positions discourage others from attacking you and invite them to support you. Sun Tzu's system teaches us how to systematically build up our positions to win success in the easiest way possible.

Competing positions are compared on the basis many elements, both objective and subjective. Sun Tzu's strategy is to identify these points of comparison and to understand how to leverage them. Learning Sun Tzu's strategy requires learning the details of how positions are compared and advanced. Sun Tzu taught that fighting to "sort things out" is a foolish way to find learn the strengths and weaknesses of a position. Conflict to tear down opposing positions is the most costly way to win competitive comparisons.

## Today's More Competitive World

In the complex, chaotic world of today, we can easily get trapped into destructive rather than productive situations. Even our smallest decisions can have huge impact on our future. The problem is that we are trained for yesterday's world of workers, not today's world of warriors. We are trained in the linear thinking of planning in predictable, hierarchical world. This thinking applies less and less to today's networked, more competitive world.

Following a plan is the worker's skill of working in pre-defined functions in an internal, stable, controlled environment. The competitive strategy of Sun Tzu is the warrior's skill of making good decisions about conditions in complex, fast-changing, competitive environments. Sun Tzu's strategic system teaches us to adapt to the unexpected events that are becoming more and more common in our lives. We live in a world where fewer and fewer key events are planned. Navigating our new world of external challenges requires a different set of skills.

Most of us make our decisions without any understanding of competition. The result is that most of us lose as many battles as we win, never making consistent progress. Events buffet us, turning us in one direction and then the other. Too often, we end up repeating our past patterns of mistakes.

The Science of Strategy Institute teaches you the warrior's skills of adaptive response. There are many organizations that teach planning and organization. The Institute is one of the few places in the world you can get learn competitive thinking, and the only place in the world, with a comprehensive Playbook.

## Seeing Situations Differently

Sun Tzu taught that a warrior's decision-making was a matter of reflex. As we develop our strategic decision-making skills, the critical conditions in situations simply "pop" out at us. This isn't magic. The latest research on how decisions are made tells us a lot about why Sun Tzu's principles work. It comes from using patterns to retrain our mind to see conditions differently. The study of successful response arose from military confrontations, where every battle clearly demonstrated how hard it is to predict events in the real world. Sun Tzu saw that winners were always those who knew how to respond appropriately to the dynamic nature of their situation.

Sun Tzu's principles provides a complete model for the key knowledge for understanding conditions in complex dynamic environments. This model "files" each piece of data into the appropriate place in the big picture. As the picture of your situation fills in, you can identify the opportunities hidden within your situation.

# Making Decisions about Conditions

Instead of focusing on a series of planned steps, Sun Tzu's principles are about making decisions regarding conditions. It concerns itself with: 1) identifying the relative strengths and weaknesses of competitive positions, 2) advancing positions leveraging opportunities, and 3) the types of responses to specific challenges that work the most frequently. Using Sun Tzu's principles, we call these three areas position awareness, opportunity development, and situation response. Each area that we master broadens your capabilities.

- Position awareness trains us to recognize that competitive situations are defined by the relationship among alternative positions. Developing this perspective never ends. It deepens throughout our lives.
- Opportunity development explores the ground, testing our perceptions. Only testing the edges of perspective through action can we know what is true.
- S ituation response trains us to recognize the key characteristics of the immediate situation and to respond appropriately. Only by practice, can we learn to trust the viewpoint we have developed.

Success in competitive environments comes from making better decisions every day. Sharp strategic reflexes flow from a clear understanding of where and when you use which competitive tools methods.

# The Key Viewpoints

As an individual, you have a unique and valuable viewpoint, but every viewpoint is inherently limited by its own position. The result is that people cannot get a useful perspective on their own situations and surrounding opportunities. The first formula of positioning awareness involve learning what information is relevant. The most advanced techniques teach how to gather that information and put it into a bigger picture.

Most people see their current situations as the sum of their past successes and failures. Too often people dwell on their mistakes while simultaneously sitting on their laurels. Sun Tzu's strategy forces you to see your position differently. How you arrived at your current position doesn't matter. Your position is what it is. It is shaped by history but history is not destiny.

In this framework, the only thing that matters is where you are going and how you are going to get there. As you begin to develop your strategic reflexes, you start to think more and more about how to secure your current position and advance it.

## Seeing the Big Picture

Most people see all the details of their lives, but they cannot see what those detail mean in terms of the big picture. As you master position awareness, you don't see your life as a point but as a path. You see your position in terms of what is changing and what resources are available. You are more aware of your ability to make decisions and your skills in working with others.

Most importantly, this strategic system forces you to get in touch with your core set of goals and values.

Untrained people usually see their life in terms of absolutes: successes and failures, good luck and bad, weakness and strength. As you begin to master position awareness, you begin to see all comparisons of strength and weakness are temporary and relative. A position is not strong or weak in itself. Its strength or weakness depends on how it compares or "fits" with surrounding positions. Weakness and strength are not what a position is, but how you use it.

## The Power of Perspective

Positional awareness gives you the specialized vocabulary you need to understanding how situations develop. Mastering this vocabulary, you begin to see the leverage points connecting past and future. You replace vague conceptions of "strength," "momentum," and "innovation" with much more pragmatic definitions that you can actually use on a day to day basis.

Mastering position awareness also changes your relationships with other people. It teaches you a different way of judging truth and character. This methods allow you to spot self-deception and dishonest in others. It also allows you to understand how you can best work with others to compensate for your different weaknesses.

Once you develop a good perspective of position, it naturally leads you to want to learn more about how you can improve you position through the various aspects of opportunity development covered in the subsequent parts of the Strategy Playbook.

## Seeing the Invisible

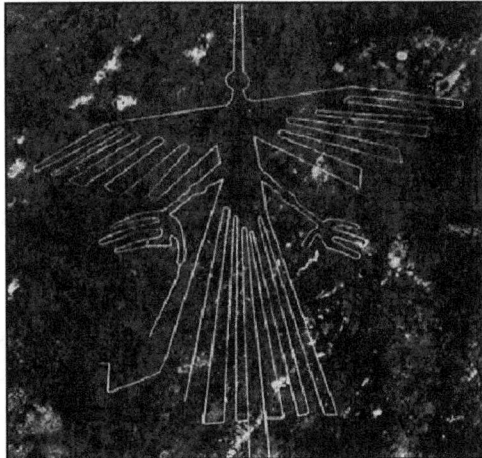

The "Nazca lines" are giant drawings etched across thirty miles of desert on Peru's southern coast. The patterns are only visible at a distance of hundreds of feet in the air. Below that, they look like strange paths or roads to nowhere. Just as we cannot see these lines without the proper perspective, people who master Sun Tzu's methods can suddenly recognize situations that were invisible to them before. Unless we have the right perspective, we cannot compare situations and positions successfully. The most recent scientific research explains why people cannot see these patterns for comparison without developing the network framework of adaptive thinking.[1]

## Seeing Patterns

We can imagine patterns in chaotic situations, but seeing real pattern is the difference between success and failure. In our seminars, we demonstrate the power of seeing patterns in a number of exercises.

The mental models used by warrior give them "situation awareness." This situation awareness isn't just vague theory. Recent research shows that it can be measured in a variety of ways.[2] We now know that untrained people fall victim to a flow of confusing information because they don't know where its pieces fit. Those trained in Sun Tzu's mental models plug this stream of information quickly and easily into a bigger picture, transforming the skeleton's provided by Sun Tzu's system into a functioning awareness of your strategic position and its relation to other positions. Each piece of information has a place in that picture. As the information comes in, it fills in the picture, like pieces of a puzzle.

The ability to see the patterns in this bigger picture allows experts in strategy to see what is invisible to most people in a number of ways. They include:

- People trained in Art of War principles--<u>recognition-primed decision-making</u> --see patterns that others do not.
- Trained people can spot anomalies, things that should happen in the network of interactions but don't.
- Trained people are in touch with changes in the environment within appropriate time horizons.
- Trained people recognize complete patterns of interconnected elements under extreme time pressure.

## Procedures Make Seeing Difficult

One of the most surprising discoveries from this research is that those who know procedures, that is, a linear view of events, alone have a ***more*** difficult time recognizing patterns than novices. An interesting study[3] examined the different recognition skills of three groups of people 1) experts, 2) novices, and 3) trainers who taught the standard procedures. The three groups were asked to pick out an expert from a group novices in a series of videos showing them performing a decision-making task, in this case, CPR. Experts were able to recognize the expert 90% of the time. Novices recognized the expert 50% of the time. The shocking fact was that trainers performed much worse that the novices, recognizing the expert only 30% of the time.

Why do those who know procedures fail to see what the experts usually see and even novices often see? Because, as research into <u>mental simulations</u> has shown, those with only a procedural model fit everything into that model and ignore elements that don't fit. In the above experiment, interviews with the trainers indicated that they assumed that the experts would always follow the procedural model. In real life, experts adapt to situations where unique conditions often trump procedure. Adapting to the situation rather than following set procedures is a central focus the form of strategy that the Institute teaches.

## Missing Expected Elements

People trained to recognize the bigger picture beyond procedures also recognize when expected elements are missing from the picture. These anomalies or, what the cognition experts [4] describe as "negative cues" are invisible to novices *and* to those trained only in procedure. Without sense of the bigger pattern, people are focused too narrowly on the problem at hand. The "dog that didn't bark" from the Sherlock Holmes story, "Silver Blaze," is the most famous example of a negative cue. Only those working from a larger nonprocedural framework can expect certain things to happen and notice when they don't.

The ability to see what is missing also comes from the expectations generated by the mental model. Process-oriented models have the expectation of one step following another, but situation-recognition models create their expectations from signals in the environment. Research [5] into the time horizons of decision-makers shows that different time scales are at work. People at the highest level of organizations must look a year or two down the road, using strategic models that work in that timeframe, doing strategic planning. Decision-makers on the front-lines, however, have to react within minutes or even seconds to changes in their situation, working from their strategic reflexes. The biggest danger is that people get so wrapped up in a process that they lose contact with their environment.

## Decisions Under Pressure

Extreme time pressure is what distinguishes front-line decision-making from strategic planners. One of the biggest discoveries in cognitive research [6] is that trained people do much better in seeing their situation instantly and making the correct decisions under time pressure. Researchers found virtually no difference between the decisions that experts made under time pressure when comparing them to decisions made without time pressure. That research also finds that those with less experience and training made dramatically worse decisions when they were put under time pressure.

The central argument for training our strategic reflexes is that our situation results, not from chance or luck, but from the instant decisions that that we all make every day. Our position is the sum of these decisions. If we cannot make the right decisions on the spot, when they are needed, our plans usually come to nothing. This is why we describe training people's strategic reflexes as helping them "do at first what most people only do at last."

The success people experience seeing what is invisible to others is dramatic. To learn more about how the strategic reflexes we teach differ from what can be planned, read about the contrast between planning and reflexes here . As our many members report, the success Sun Tzu's system makes possible is remarkable.

1 Chi, Glaser, & Farr, 1988, The Nature of Expertise, Erlbaum
2 Endsley & Garland, Analysis and Measurement of Situation Awareness
3 Klein & Klein, 1981, "Perceptual/Cognitive Analysis of proficient CPR Performance", Midwestern Psychological Association Meeting, Chicago.
4 Dr. David Noble, Evidence Based Research, Inc.In Gary Klein, Sources of Power, 1999
5 Jacobs & Jaques, 1991, "Executive Leadership".In Gal & Mangelsdofs (eds.), Handbook of Military Psychology, Wiley
6 Calder, Klein, Crandall,1988, "Time Pressure, Skill, and Move Quality in Chess". American Journal of Psychology, 101:481-493

# About Perspective

Sun Tzu's science of strategy is, above all, an information science. Sun Tzu realized that the most important weapon in competition was the human mind. In Volume Two of the *Art of War Playbook*, we look at Sun Tzu's principles regarding the use of information. In his view, information shifts radically depending on the perspective from which one view it. These differences of perspective are one of the keys to creating powerful competitive strategies.

Today's new media brings us a flood of information, but the problem is that this information makes decision-making more difficult. Without the perspective that Sun Tzu provides, identifying what is important is like finding a needle in a haystack. The value of Sun Tzu's strategy is that its methods are designed to work where we know we can never have all the key information we need. Its methods are like a magnet pulling a few of the critical pieces of information from that haystack.

In a controlled environment, inside an organization, good information, especially about the plans of others, ensures good predictions about the future. However, in the larger, competitive environment, you cannot predict the future [1]*. Your position inside your company may seem secure, but in a marketplace customers are free to decide what they do. This means that while you may be able to predict that you can make a cake, you cannot predict that anyone in the marketplace will buy it.

In reality, we operate with incomplete information [2]* as a matter of course. Competitive environments are filled with misinformation. They are filled with outdated information. The limitations of information affect buyers as well as sellers. Our only guide to the future in competitive environments is the past. And while there is some continuity with the past, new alternatives are constantly being offered.

We can make decisions based only upon our subjective impressions [2]*. The less information we have, the more our subjective impressions differ from the physical reality. In chess, opposing players have access to all relevant information except each others' plans. In real-life competition, some people have information that others don't have. No matter how good our inside information, by definition we are outsiders to most of the world.

The strategic method [3] first gathers as much relevant information as quickly as possible. They then quickly filter that information so that actions can be taken safely, but each move is a probe designed to test our information and gain additional information that we could not have gotten without action. The final step is recognizing both our successes and failures.

## Predicting the Future

In a controlled environment inside an organization, good information, especially about the plans of others, ensures good information about the future. The best way to predict the future is to create it. If you have a proven plan and access to the right ingredients, equipment, and skills, you can predict what your plan will create. For example, if you have a cake recipe, access to a kitchen, the necessary ingredients, and the time to make it, you can usually correctly predict that the future will have one more cake in it.

This is prediction is only possible because you control the process. You control the resources and the actions of those involved. This defines a controlled environment.

However, you cannot predict the actions of others and their use of their resources in the larger, competitive environment. In a marketplace, for example, customers are free to decide what they do. They control the key resource involved, their money. This means that while you may be able to predict that you can make a cake, you cannot predict that anyone in the marketplace will buy it.

In a competitive environment, you do not have access to the information that other people are using to make their future decisions. The environment is too large and complex. You often do not even know who the relevant actors in that environment are, much less the information that they have access to. When a business opens its doors in the morning, it doesn't know who, if anyone, will walk through them. Even if we could read each other's minds, there are simply too many people and possibilities to manage the vast amount of information involved.

We live in a flood of information. More information doesn't make the future more predictable. It makes the possibilities of the future even more confusing. In a controlled environment, the more information we have, the better our sense of control. However, in a dynamic, competitive environment, more information is just more noise.

The mental models taught by traditional strategy are designed to put a flood of information into a context where decisions can be made without a perfect knowledge of the future. Without these models, it is impossible to filter out what information is relevant in a given situation and what is just noise.

## Incomplete Information

In competitive environments, we operate with incomplete information as a matter of course. No battle in history would ever have been fought if people had good information about their relative strengths. Both sides would know before the battle who would win. Battles are fought only because both sides think they can win.

Someone is wrong. At the most, only one side can be right. Both sides are often wrong when we consider the cost and value of most battles.

But no one knows who will win in competition. The information any group has is an insignificant portion of the total information in the environment. Getting all the information you need to bake a cake in a controlled environment is relatively easy. Getting all the information you need to sell cakes in the competitive market is much more difficult. There are always too many variables. There are always too many unknowns. Who can know how many people will decide they want to buy a cake today? Many who buy cakes in the afternoon didn't even have that information themselves in the morning.

Competitive environments are also filled with misinformation. Competitors try to mislead each other regarding not only their future plans but their current circumstances. Individuals distort the truth for a variety of reasons. As in a game of poker, any advantage you have is linked to what you know that the other players don't know.

The limitations of information affect a buyer as well as a seller. Internal resources are resources about which we have good information. We do not have good information about external resources, that is, the resources that others have. This makes finding the best product, the lowest-cost supplier, or a reliable service provider a challenge. The volume of unknown information in the external market is always much more than the known information available to any single decision-maker.

In controlled environments, everyone is relatively well informed about what is changing. In larger, more complex, competitive environments, it is infinitely more difficult to keep up with increasingly fast-changing information.

The past does not predict the future in competitive environments. Neither does planning. Conditions are fluid. New alternatives are constantly being offered. Everyone is continuously reacting to the changes around them, creating dynamic situations. Everyone predicts success, but actual results are unpredictable.

When people are successful, they think their planning worked. When they fail, they blame their plans. Most fail to see the effects of strategy because they don't understand the differences between strategy and planning.

## Subobjective Information

Among the many powerful ideas that Sun Tzu teaches is that reality is always different than our subjective perceptions of it. We cannot know objective reality without filtering through our mental models. What is usually translated as "deception" in Sun Tzu's work is better described as the awareness that there is always a difference between perception and reality, but that we must deal with both at once, learning to make good decisions on "subobjective information."

## Decisions Based on Perceptions

People make decisions based upon conditions, but everyone's idea of conditions is only based upon their subjective impressions. The less information we have, the more our subjective impressions differ from the physical reality. The fewer information sources we have and the more alike those information sources are, the narrower our perspective. The more information sources we have and the more variety in those sources, the broader our perspective.

"Insider" information is information about a situation that is held exclusively by one person or group of people. Insider information usually refers to information available only to those who are in a specific position. Outsiders are not privy to it. In chess, opposing players have access to all relevant information except each other's plans. This means that chess has very little insider information. This is very different from a contest such as poker, where each player has access to information about his or her own hand that no one else has. In real-life competition, insider information is critical to future events, but by definition most people do not have it.

## Measures of Position

There are no absolute values in strategy. All judgments about positions are relative. These judgments are made by individuals from their own subjective perspective. There is no such thing as an objective condition that we call "strength." Strength and weakness are determined by comparing positions. From that comparison, we identify positions we suspect are stronger and weaker in one area or another. However, our judgments about conditions must be tested. Based upon that test, we can then say that various aspects of those positions are relatively stronger or weaker.

In these relative comparisons, insider information is always in play. We may have insider information about our own positions, but we do not have insider information about the positions that we are using for comparison. So no matter how good our inside information, we are always making decisions out of ignorance.

## Sun Tzu's Strategic Method

How can we make good strategic decisions in an instant with limited information? Sun Tzu's Warrior's principles teach a number of sophisticated and yet practical models for decision making.

Knowing What is Relevant

Everything in Sun Tzu's strategy revolves around the idea of positioning. The only relevant question is: how do we advance our position? Our positions in all competitive arenas are determined by our decisions about conditions. Since information about conditions is critical to decisions, the first formulas of strategy are those designed to gather and organize as much relevant information as possible. By its nature, the environment frustrates information gathers. On one hand, it provides more information than we can handle. On the other, it seeks to hide the most critical information in a flood of data. Therefore, the tools of strategy limit our data collection to what is key and use methods that give us at least some insight into what we do not know. The concept of positioning is designed to limit the gathering of information to certain key areas where useful information can be found.

## Focusing on Opportunities

The direction of positions is determined by motivation. What is an opportunity? It depends on our goal. Opportunities are determined by the opening that take us most easily toward our goals. The next formulas in Sun Tzu's strategy filter information to identify those openings so that decisions about actions can be made. This step requires its own specialized set of tools used for identifying opportunities and evaluating them. The process of advancing a position identifies the most likely areas where an advance can be made.

As Will Rogers once said, "It isn't what we don't know that gives us trouble. It's what we know that ain't so." Because each move is an experiment, Sun Tzu's first priority is experimenting safely. For example, the Minimizing Mistakes Formula teaches that initial moves should be small, limited, and local because they are the least risky.

Each move is a probe designed to test information in real time and determine its value. In making these moves, however, we must adapt to the situation as we find it. This systematic testing requires its own toolkit for adapting our experiments to the conditions we discover in the environment and that we can only discover by attempting something. Each strategic move seeks to make progress in a certain direction, but the immediate path to progress is discovered in the process of making the move.

## Every Failure Is a Success

We win some and we learn some. If our goal is gaining a better understanding of our position, every exploration is successful. This requires recognizing both our successes and failures. As Thomas Edison recognized, most experiments fail. However, if conducted correctly, even failed experiments are helpful because they give you good information. Every move is successful in the sense of improving your quality of information about the competitive environment.

Though we must be prepared for failure, we live for success. We can often find success, however small, in every move. The final step is claiming our new position. Even when we have just gained knowledge, we have advanced our position in that aspect. These are the tools necessary to get every drop of value from a new position.

## Developing Perspective

Given the proper methods, the chaotic nature of the environment becomes our ally. Sun Tzu's strategy doesn't change environmental conditions, but it changes our decisions in response to them. Small increases in the quality of our decisions can, over time, make huge differences in our position.

Our goal isn't understanding all the complexities affecting a situation. That power is beyond our capabilities. However, we can see the situation better than those around us. That is always our goal in developing our perspective. We use everyone's else's viewpoint to construct a more comprehensive big picture.

Many of the techniques first developed by Sun Tzu and developed over time allow us to use the shortage of information to our advantage. It is always easier and less expensive to control a situation by controlling the flow of information than by using physical force. For example, you create strategic momentum by introducing new information into the environment when you are prepared for it and your opponents are not.

# 2.0.0 Developing Perspective

Sun Tzu seven key methods for adding depth to competitive analysis.

*"Discover an opportunity by listening.*
*Adjust to your situation.*
*Get assistance from the outside."*

Sun Tzu's The Art of War 1:3:-1-3

*"The manager has a short-range view; the leader has a long-range perspective."*

Warren G. Bennis

**General Principle:** A strategic perspective requires systematically gathering outside opinions and facts.

## Situation:

One person's perspective is narrow, seeing only one side of a situation. Our view of *our own* position is myopic. We are too close to our own lives to see them clearly. This makes comparing alternatives difficult. Adding to this problem, we naturally know, meet, and befriend people much like ourselves. Our "natural" networks are poorly suited from developing strategic perspective. Natural groups largely share the same perspective. Our friends and family see the world from more or less the same angle that we do. Our friends tend to be the same age and have the same background and interests. They usually share our opinions on a number of topics.

## Opportunity:

Each person's opportunities are unique. Sun Tzu's principles teach us how to get the information we need to discover our opportunities. They are designed to filter information. Sun Tzu's methods of gathering information and creating contact networks seek to overcome their natural problems with having a narrow perspective. His key methods for information creates the well-rounded strategic perspective that helps us see the opportunities hidden in our situation. Sun Tzu's strategy tells us where to find those hidden opportunities.

## Key Methods:

These are the seven key methods for developing perspective.

*1. Our decisions are only as good as our information.* The gathering of quality information is not tangential to making good decisions. It is a core skill. By definition, a good strategist is someone who is skilled at getting the right information at the right time. The goal of gathering information in Sun Tzu's strategy is the development of perspective. Perspective is the ability to see situations as completely and objectively as possible. A complete perspective is a perspective that sees a situation from as many different sides as possible (2.1 Information Value).

*2. Developing a broad perspective requires systematic information gathering.* We need specific forms of information. We all acquire information naturally in the process of living our lives. This natural information seldom meets our criteria for valuable information. Much of Sun Tzu's system is designed to address the challenges of getting the right information we need in chaotic competitive environments at the right time. To do so, we need a specific type of contact network and to use it to identify valuable information (2.2 Information Gathering).

*3. Our information is only as good as our personal interactions.* While information today is available from all types of sources, Sun Tzu focuses primarily on direct human contact. Only the human brain can compile information into a valuable form. All written and stored information was originally developed by people. Sun Tzu wants us to develop first-hand sources who can think specifically about our situation. In the world of direct relationships, we don't always get information directly. Our most valuable information comes from action, that is, seeing how people react to our actions (2.3 Personal Interactions).

*4. We need five different types of contact to form a complete network.* These contacts represent the five elements that define a competitive position. Our contact network is limited by our ability to organize and communicate competitive information. Bigger networks are not inherently better because of the costs of maintaining them. We are looking for more complete networks. One of the advantages of Sun Tzu's system is that it defines the key elements needed to understand our situations (2.4 Contact Networks).

*5. To organize detailed information into a comprehensive picture we need distance.* In developing our contacts, we want contacts who are close enough to a situation to get detailed information. We also need contacts who are distant enough from our situations to get perspective on them. Distance gives us a bigger picture, but the more distant we are from a situation, the more key details we miss. We need both detailed and generalized information on our competitive position. Our goal is to create a comprehensive picture of the situation (2.5 The Big Picture).

*6. We gather information with the goal of creating leverage.* Information is not valuable in and of itself. There is an infinite supply of information. Our information search must focus specifically on the types of information that give us leverage. This is information where subjective perspectives can be transformed into tangible positions (2.6 Knowledge Leverage).

*7. **Knowledge value and secrecy go hand in hand, both requiring the other**. This means that they are complementary opposites in Sun Tzu's system. The more public information is, the less valuable it is. The more private information is, the more valuable it is (2.7 Information Secrecy).

## Illustration:

Let us illustrate these ideas by looking at the situation of a typical small business owner.

*1. **Our decisions are only as good as our information**. Small business owners find themselves in trouble when events catch them unaware. If an employee quits, a supplier runs out of products, or the city decides to tear up their street, they are in trouble if they don't hear about it until the day it happens.

*2. **Developing a broad perspective requires systematic information gathering**. It doesn't matter if we run a restaurant, a grocery store, or a tattoo parlor, we are in the information business. ***Our information is only as good as our personal interactions***. We can only hear about future plans of employees, suppliers, or the city if we are talking to the people who know those plans. The earlier we know, the more of an impact we can have. They may not tell us directly what we need to know, so we have to discern it from our interactions with them.

*3. **We need five different types of contact to form a complete network**. It doesn't matter if we run a restaurant, a grocery store, or a tattoo parlor, we need information about the business climate, the customer marketplace, the lives of those we depend on, knowledge of methods in our industry, and knowledge of people's goals and values.

*4. **To organize detailed information into a comprehensive picture we need distance**. We need information about the local business climate and the nation's business climate. We need knowledge about methods in our specific niche and knowledge of new technology that affects everyone. ***We gather information with the goal of creating leverage***. It doesn't matter if we run a restaurant, a grocery store, or a tattoo parlor, the new idea that takes our business to the next level will come from our information network.

**5. *Knowledge value and secrecy go hand in hand, both requiring the other.*** We must know which information that we need to communicate to attract customers and which information we must keep secret to maintain a competitive advantage.

# 2.1 Information Value

Sun Tzu's six key methods regarding knowledge and communication as the basis of strategy.

*"The military commander's knowledge is the key. It determines if the civilian officials can govern. It determines if the nation's households are peaceful or a danger to the state."*

Sun Tzu's The Art of War 2:5:-3-5

*"Information is a source of learning. But unless it is organized, processed, and available to the right people in a format for decision making, it is a burden, not a benefit."*

William Pollard

**General Principle:** Strategy depends on acquiring and using information to control situations.

## Situation:

Our perception of reality is less than perfect. Our senses capture reality in an incomplete form. Our thoughts only partly comprehend what we sense. We must interpret what we see and hear. We organize that information based on very imperfect models of how the world really works. In a sense, we do not live in reality. We live in our limited perceptions and models of reality. Mistaking our perception for reality can be extremely dangerous. Since we all live within these limitations, information that goes outside of common perception and models is extremely valuable.

## Opportunity:

Because we all live in our private worlds of perceptions, we all have the opportunity of finding unique advantages. We use information directly in two basic ways to create an advantage. First, we try to understand the true hidden nature of reality a little better than others with whom we are dealing. Second, we try to change people's perceptions so that they make decisions that give us an advantage for their own advantage. Our environment is rich in information, but our advantages do not come from more information but from better mental models for filtering and organizing that information. This is particularly easy in a world where people see only what is under control. We live on small islands of control in a vast sea of chaos. Control is the exception. Chaos is the larger reality.

## Key Methods:

Sun Tzu's strategy was specifically defined to give us better mental models for accurately interpreting the strategic significance of the events that we witness. Many of these models were developed because people naturally confuse what they see happening in strategic encounters because much of what actually happens is non-intuitive. We must start with a basic understanding of what information is and why it is valuable.

*1. We must identify valuable information out of too much information.* Our information comes from our ability to discern differences between conditions. We experience events when we see, hear, smell, taste, and feel something change in our environment.

We cannot experience everything at once, even in our immediate proximity, so we are always filtering information. Because we cannot capture everything, we try to let what is valuable in while filtering out what is unimportant (Information Limits).

**2. *Valuable information is filtered and organized by imperfect mental models.*** Our minds convert immediate sensory experiences into generalized, symbolic forms. This generalized symbolic knowledge can be stored, shared with others, and duplicated. Direct sensory information cannot be stored, duplicated and shared in a similarly useful way. Language in the form of writing allows us to preserve and communicate information through time. Symbolic knowledge is organized to create our mental models. Our mental models are meta-information, information about information. They describes the principles that we use to understand how the environment operates (2.2.2 Mental Models).

**3. *Uncertainty is what makes information valuable.*** If we knew the future, we wouldn't need information. Our uncertainty drives us to want to learn more. What we see can be misleading, as anyone who has attended a magic show knows. Given that our mental models are imperfect, we are always imperfect witnesses. We are in a constant state of tension and attention because we want to know what the future will bring. New information can either confirm or violate our expectations of knowledge (2.1.2 Leveraging Uncertainty).

**4. *All preserved information about events grows less valuable over time.*** When we talk about the "information revolution," we are referring to the ability of modern technology to allow us to more easily capture information, duplicate it, and communicate it. All such preserved information is about the past. The information is used to create the mental models through which we predict the future. Our predictions about the future are based on outdated information from the past. These models work only because certain fundamental aspects of reality persist over time. Preserving and communicating information raises questions about when information is outdated. Many statements about conditions are time-sensitive. What was once true is not necessarily still true right now (1.8.3 Cycle Time).

**5. The value of information arises from the fact that all communication is guided by solely selfinterest.** Our ability to communicate with others depends upon the symbols that we share with them. We share information and keep information secret based upon what we see as our self interest. Information that is broadly known has a very different type of value than information that only a few people know. We are all constantly using information to our advantage. Even people who always tell the truth do so because they want the advantage of being known as truthful. Communicating information was once limited to the speed of human travel. Thanks to electronic media, duplication of information is virtually free and communication virtually instantaneous. (2.1.3 Strategic Deception).

**6. Surprise breaks through limitations, mental models, and uncertainty to create new value.** The ability to surprise and to be surprised is the wild card in the information deck. For the last two hundred years, people have begun to appreciate the value of radically new ideas. In productive environments, surprise is negative. In competitive environments, it represents an opening to new opportunities (2.1.4 Surprise).

## Illustration:

Let us illustrate these ideas in a confusing, self-referencing form, dealing with you reading this site right now.

**1. We must identify valuable information out of too much information.** There are millions of pages that you could have accessed on the Internet, but if you are reading this now, you are doing so because you think it is more valuable than anything else you could find right now.

**2. Valuable information is filtered and organized by imperfect mental models.** You are seeing this word now through a mental model of language. If you cannot read English, you cannot understand this. These words are just symbols for shared ideas. When you start reading about a "fringlimest," you cannot understand what you are reading because it isn't part of your model. It is a nonsense word.

**3. Uncertainty is what makes information valuable.** Something is happening inside your computer right now, but you cannot see what it is. Real events are taking place in your room right now, but these words control you because you see them as important to your future. You are reading because you want to master the techniques for using the uncertainty of the world.

**4. All preserved information about events grows less valuable over time.** This sentence has been on the server for months. Is it still important? It is an event for you now, but it describes a timeless concept not a real world event. As you are reading this, the above sentence is old but is it outdated?

**5. The value of information arises from the fact that all communication is guided by solely self interest.** I am writing this sentence out of self-interest. I want to inspire you to learn more about Sun Tzu. However, just because this information is in my self interest doesn't mean that it isn't in your best interest as well.

**6. Surprise breaks through limitations, mental models, and uncertainty to create new value.** Surprise! I have nothing more to say.

# 2.1.1 Information Limits

Sun Tzu's eight key methods for making good decisions with limited information.

*"Knowledge is victory. No knowledge, no victory."*
Sun Tzu's The Art of War 1:1:36-37 (Ancient Chinese Revealed Version)

*"Be willing to make decisions. That's the most important quality in a good leader."*
General George S. Patton

**General Principle:** Strategic decisions are always made with limited information.

## Situation:

We must be realistic about the quality of competitive information. There is an infinite amount of information that may be relevant to our competitive position. Much of this information is not only unknown but unknowable. The chain that brings us information consists of weak links. Unexpected events continually come from unforeseen directions. Information about these events is always limited. Our impressions about what is happening is filtered through our expectations, which are too often wrong. Sensory information is limited, not only by our senses, but by our focus and attention. Our mental models can filter out the wrong information. Our words never clearly express our ideas. Information is lost in communication: what is said is not necessarily what is heard. More information is lost in interpretation: what is meant is not necessarily what others think is meant.

## Opportunity:

Despite the limitation of quality information, we must make decisions. The more quickly we make them, the better. We can gather only as much information as time allows. Many key decisions must be made in an instant. The time limits on making decisions is a key factor limiting our information about a situation (1.8.3 Cycle Time). While having better information than others is always beneficial, better information is seldom required to make better decisions than most people. All we need is better knowledge of what the key information is and a clearer focus on it than others (1.7.2 Goal Focus).

## Key Methods:

Since complete and accurate information is never going to be available, we have to look at information differently in order to make our decisions. Good strategic decisions can be made with limited information, but only if we know the appropriate methods. To use those methods, we must:

*1. We make good decisions ith limited information by comparing the relative value of making a decision against that of making no decision.* If we have nothing much to gain or nothing much to lose, we should avoid acting on information. Action is always costly. Just having information doesn't demand that we act upon it. We must ask ourselves, "Does a decision really need to be made now?" (4.2 Choosing Non-Action)

*2. We make good decisions with limited information by estimating the cost of making the wrong decision.* The potential value of a decision is only half the equation. We make wrong decisions all the time because we don't have perfect information about the future. Wrong decisions are invaluable learning tools. We must ask ourselves, "Is any decision based on this information safe if the information is wrong?" (3.1 Strategic Economics)

*3. We make good decisions with limited information by ignoring information that doesn't impact the decision.* In Sun Tzu's system, we use the five elements to give us a solid guide. A vast majority of information related to a decision or situation doesn't affect our decision one way or another. If information doesn't impact one of the five key elements, such information can be very interesting, even distracting, arousing our curiosity, but that doesn't make it relevant. When information does touch on one of the key elements, the first question we should ask is: "If this information were different, would it change my decision?" (1.3 Elemental Analysis)

*4. We make good decisions with limited information by weighing information based upon its relative importance to the decision.* In competition, everything is a comparison. All the remaining information affects our decision, but not all of it is equal in its impact. We must ask, "Which information is most influencing my decision?" (1.3.1 Competitive Comparison)

*5. We make good decisions with limited information by testing information consistency against our situation awareness.* People often are influenced by the worst and most inconsistent information simply because it demands attention. However, that characteristic doesn't make it true. We must ask ourselves, given all we know about the situation and its history, is this information likely to be true?" (6.1 Situation Recognition)

**6. We make good decisions with limited information by always suspecting that inconsistent information is wrong.** Our information can be wrong because 1) it was garbled in communication, 2) events were misinterpreted, 3) people intentionally want to mislead us through secrecy or deception, or 4) the information has been outdated by more recent developments. We must ask ourselves, "How could this information be incorrect or how can it be quickly verified?" (2.1.3 Strategic Deception)

**7. We make good decisions with limited information by balancing the cost of collecting more information against value of quick action.** Action might be the quickest and least costly way to get better information. Often, it is the only way to get better information. If reliable, relevant information can be gathered more quickly and easily without action, we should gather it, but decisions can always be avoided by using the excuse that more information must be gathered. We must ask ourselves, "Is action the fastest and least expensive way to find out the truth?" (3.1.2 Strategic Profitability)

**8. We make good decisions with limited information by having a prejudice toward acting to learn more.** The best way to get better information is often through action not passing inquiry. Situations always change. It is a fantasy to think that we can always gather enough information to always make the right decision. If action is the best decision now, it is best to act now before the situation changes. We must ask ourselves, "Why wait?" The answer must never be, "For more information." (5.3.1 Speed and Quickness)

## Illustration:

Let us use the example of gathering information about someone with who we are considering a serious relationship. The same principles work whether the relationship is personal or professional.

*1. We make good decisions with limited information by comparing the relative value of making a decision against that of making no decision.* If we do not see a great deal of potential value in the relationship, we should generally avoid it.

*2. We make good decisions with limited information by estimating the cost of making the wrong decision.* If rejecting the relationship is more costly than accepting it, we must consider that in our decision.

*3. We make good decisions with limited information by ignoring information that doesn't impact the decision.* Even if true, most past behavior in other relationships, good or bad, will have little impact on our future relationship.

*4. We make good decisions with limited information by weighing information based upon its relative importance to the decision.* We must know what is important in the relationship and which information that we have relates most directly to our values.

*5. We make good decisions with limited information by testing information consistency against our situation awareness.* Our picture of the person should come from all our information and, especially, from our direct, first-hand experiences. Most information should be consistent with a single picture. We must not fool ourselves, pretending that the general picture tells the story that we want to hear as opposed to the one we need to know.

*6. We make good decisions with limited information by always suspecting that inconsistent information is wrong.* Information about a person that seems out-of-character from our first-hand experiences should be immediately suspect rather than immediately believed.

***7. We make good decisions with limited information by balancing the cost of collecting more information against value of quick action.*** In some situations, a closer relationship will generate more information than outside research. In others, outside research is a least costly path.

***8. We make good decisions with limited information by having a prejudice toward acting to learn more.*** If is always better to say either "Yes" or "No" to the relationship than have it linger in limbo. Either path allows us to move forward, while making no decision leaves us stuck.

# 2.1.2 Leveraging Uncertainty

Sun Tzu's five key methods for leveraging the elemental nature of uncertainty.

*Chaos gives birth to control."*
*Fear gives birth to courage."*
*Weakness gives birth to strength."*
Sun Tzu's The Art of War 5:4:7-9

*"Confusion is a word we have invented for an order which is not yet understood."*
Henry Miller

**General Principle:** Strategic decisions are always made with limited information.

## Situation:

All our early experiences in life are in controlled environments, where we are protected from competitive chaos. We are raised and educated in environments where the future is predictable and the information that we need most is readily available. In our first jobs outside the home, we only have to follow directions and do as we are told. These early experiences create false expectation of certainty. When we venture out from controlled environments into competitive environments, our mental model of a world in control is violated. We make the painful discovery that much of what happens is outside of anyone's control and unpredictable. Many of us can never accept this view of reality. We constantly yearn for the comfortable mindset of our childhood rather than get comfortable with uncertainty.

## Opportunity:

Our opportunity comes from knowing that competitive situations always have hidden opportunities. No matter how certain, solid, or predictable the world seems, there are always new possibilities hidden in plain sight. Most people are untrained and unprepared for the fact. This gives us an advantage. We can train our mind to find new possibilities in what confuses others. We are all confused by the information that we get, but those who expect information to be reliable, complete, and what we expect miss what is possible. Instead of trying to "fix" the problem of making decisions with incomplete and inaccurate information by attempting to get perfect information, we can leverage the uncertainty of situations and of others. An expectation of uncertainty gives us a relative advantage in every situation (1.3.1 Competitive Comparison).

## Key Methods:

We leverage uncertainty by understanding its inherent potential in every key element that defines a competitive position.

*1. We leverage the fuzziness of values and goal to create shared missions.* The opposing nature of goals that create rivals and enemies is uncertain and incomplete. We must avoid seeing situations in terms of black and white. Instead we look for areas of gray where we can find shared missions hidden in what appears to be conflicting situations (1.6.1 Shared Mission).

*2. We leverage the uncertain direction of climate by seeing people's confusion as an opportunity.* Most people fear change. They often fear it. Sun Tzu teaches us to embrace it because it is the source of all opportunities. Let others waste their resources trying to stop change. We adapt to change and surf on the waves of change. A constant opportunity in change is using it as a reason to change people's mind. New events require new decisions. By embracing change, we can leverage our superior knowledge against the confusions and uncertainty of others (1.4.1 Climate Shift).

*3. We leverage the uncertainties of ground to utilize hidden resources.* Our rivals expect us to use our obvious resources. Not all of our resources are obvious, even to us. We can easily overlook the potential of our resources. We must develop the mindset of automatically thinking about how we can utilize every resources that we control (1.4.2 Ground Features).

*4. We leverage the uncertainties of character by expecting pressure to bring out the best and worst in people.* Sun Tzu teaches that people's strengths of character are also the source of their weakness. When people are put under pressure, slight flaws can lead to them either cracking or breaking out (1.5.1 Command Leadership).

*5. We leverage the uncertainties of methods by expecting the probable but being ready for the unlikely.* We live in a world of probabilities, not certainties. While Sun Tzu teaches us to learn and use the most likely paths of competition, his teaching prepares us for what is highly unlikely. We avoid risking everything, even when the odds are in our favor because the unlikely will eventually happen. We are awake to uncommon opportunities because they will eventually happen as well ( 1.8.4 Probabilistic Process).

## Illustration:

Let us illustrate these principles in a variety of competitive arenas.

*1. We leverage the fuzziness of values and goal to create shared missions*. Politicians constantly miss potential common ground because they see every situation in terms of partisan enmity.

*2. We leverage the uncertain direction of climate by expecting the creation of new opportunities.* In the world of technology, the confusion about new technology creates opportunities for high-tech companies. Some of the most successful firms in hi-tech didn't have the best technology, but they were able to leverage people's uncertainty, their hopes and fears regarding technology, better than others.

*3. We leverage the uncertainties of ground to utilize hidden resources*. During an agricultural age, land with oil was once considered a liability because it couldn't be farmed. Seeing the potential in oil required seeing the world from a different perspective.

*4. We leverage the uncertainties of character by expecting pressure to bring out the best and worst in people.* Capt. Chesley "Sully" Sullenberger always had the same character. He wasn't heralded as a *hero* until he successfully landed a crippled US Airways flight in the Hudson.

*5. We leverage the uncertainties of methods by expecting the probable but being ready for the unlikely.* Bill Gates ran a software company that sold programming languages when the opportunity arose to offer an operating system for the first IBM PC. This wasn't the opportunity he expected, but it was the one that he used. Even if we don't use this technique ourselves, we have to be constantly aware of when it is being used against us. It is more common than most people realize. We leverage uncertainty by understanding its inherent potential in every key element that defines a competitive position.

## 2.1.3 Strategic Deception

Sun Tzu nine key methods in misinformation and disinformation in competition.

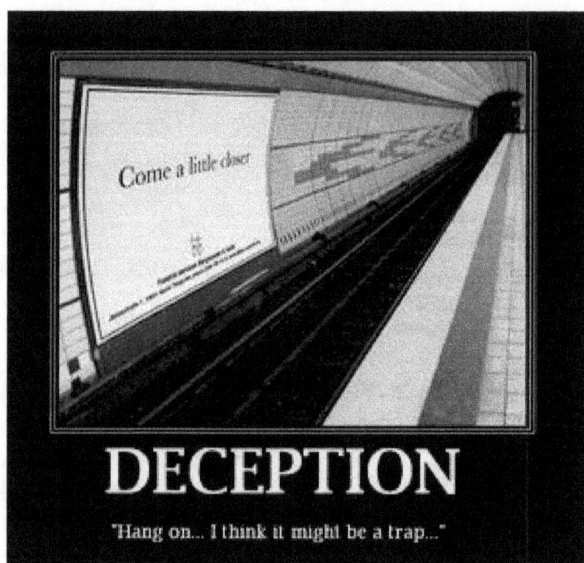

Come a little closer

DECEPTION

"Hang on... I think it might be a trap..."

*"Warfare is one thing.*
*It is a philosophy of deception."*
Sun Tzu's The Art of War 1:4:1-2

*"Now I believe I can hear the philosophers protesting*
*that it can only be misery to live in folly, illusion,*
*deception and ignorance, but it isn't --it's human."*
Desiderius Erasmus

**General Principle:** Misinformation and disinformation are competitive tools.

## Situation:

Knowledge is limited. Situations are uncertain. Nothing is more uncertain than what is hidden in the human heart. We are always seeking to shape the views of others to reach our personal objectives. From the time we are children, we recognize that we can control situations by controlling the information that others get about those situations. The point is that perception is not reality, but by controlling perception, people can control reality. Information does not necessarily reflect any objective reality at all but what others want us to think about reality.

## Opportunity:

Information is valuable, and it is less costly to advance our position using information that it is using other resources. Physically changing a position is usually more costly than changing the subjective view of positions. By changing the viewpoints of others, we can physically advance our position more easily. Opinions change outcomes just as outcomes change opinions. Our ability to leverage information to advance a position inexpensively is the core of Sun Tzu's strategy. The point is that, since no one knows the ultimate truth, we have to think about the best way to represent situations in order to create a certain set of expectations. We are judged against the expectations that we create as much as we are by objective outcomes.

## Key Methods:

Sun Tzu principles regarding the use of misinformation and disinformation are both a prescription and a warning. We must not only be willing to use these information tools as the situation demands, but we must also be constantly suspicious of the character of the information we are getting.

*1. The possibility of deception must be considered in every competitive situation*. Deception means nothing more than manipulating information to our advantage. When making decisions, we can never take information at face value. We must constantly ask ourselves how others might be using information to manipulate us or we might use a given situation to manipulate others (1.2 Subobjective Positions).

*2. Deception can misrepresent conditions or motivations.* Actions are always interpreted in light of the presumed purpose behind them. Misrepresentation of facts are easier to disprove than misrepresentations of motivations. Facts are external while motivation is internal. It is harder to prove a philosophy wrong than a simple fact (1.6.2 Types of Motivations).

*3. Misinformation distorts the conditions of a situation.* It does this by exaggerating or minimizing aspects of the situations. This can be intentional due to self-interest or accidental due to lack of knowledge. In Sun Tzu's system, we must misinformation to mean "missing information." Since all information is limited, all information is, to one degree or another, misinformation and must be evaluated in that light. Misinformation emphasizes some facts over others or leaves out critical details that impact a situation (2.1.1 Information Limits).

*4. We must consider people's perspective and motivations when we interpret information from them*. As we have said, misinformation can be created intentionally or unintentionally. People naturally create or pass on misinformation because it supports their position while leaving out or minimizing aspects that hurt their position. Thus, misinformation can represent their honest viewpoint, even when wrong. Information must always be judged by its source and especially their motivations. We automatically put information in the light that benefits us the most (1.6 Mission Values)

*5. The biggest danger is not others deceiving us, but that we deceive ourselves.* There is always a temptation to believe what we want to believe. We easily filter out information that runs contrary to our perspective and desires. The most destructive form of deception is always self-deception (2.0 Developing Perspective).

**6. Disinformation is information that represents a condition as the opposite of what it is.** The "big lie " is often more powerful and even believable than the slight lie. It is can be daring enough to cause us to drop our natural suspicions about misinformation. It can be grand enough to alter our perspective entirely. Disinformation works because of extreme situations naturally tend to reverse themselves. Sun Tzu recommends the constant use of disinformation in the first chapter of *The Art of War*. Many of the principles for using information to make strategic decisions are designed to avoid falling into the trap of disinformation (3.2.5 Dynamic Reversal).

**7. Deception is used to create expectations in others.** Those expectations affect both decisions and opinions. The same actions are evaluated very differently depending upon the expectations created. Depending on the mindset that we create, our actions can either disappoint or please people based on the level of their expectations (2.1.4 Surprise).

**8. The advantages of deception must be balanced against its impact on credibility.** Success requires the support of others. That support is impossible to get if we are not trusted. Deception can be used to create trust, such as when we under-promise and over deliver, as well as to destroy trust (1.6.1 Shared Mission).

**9. All opinions are eventually measured against objective outcomes.** This is why strategy teaches us to judge people by their actions and not by their words. Actions can still be designed to mislead us, but actions require more investment. As the old saying goes, "Talk is cheap." So information has both a short-term effect, creating expectations, ***and*** a long-term effect, when those expectations are evaluated in light of following events. We cannot consider the total effect of using information or misinformation without factoring in both the short-term and the long-term (1.8.1 Creation and Destruction).

# Illustration:

Let us illustrate these principles in a variety of competitive arenas.

*1. The possibility of deception must be considered in every competitive situation*. The car salesperson may or may not know whether or not the car is a lemon, but his sales pitch is the same regardless of his knowledge.

*2. Deception can misrepresent conditions or motivations*. A car salesperson can be more concerned with his immediate commissions or with having repeat customers in the future. The first type of salesperson will misrepresent the facts intentionally, while the second type will do so only accidentally.

*3. Misinformation distorts the conditions of a situation*. Since a salesperson has chosen to work for a given car company, he or she begins with the belief in the superiority of that product, whether or not the belief is justified.

*4. We must consider people's perspective and motivations when we interpret information from them*. A car salesperson can provide lots of solid information, but his or her information about competing products is likely to have gaps that favor his or her own products.

*5. The biggest danger is not others deceiving us, but that we deceive ourselves.* It is not what the salesperson says, but what we want to believe. We may believe that a given model of car will make us more popular when, in fact, it has no such effect.

*6. Disinformation represents a condition to be the opposite of what it is.* Some cars were own by little, old ladies who drove them only once a week. Most are not.

*7. Deception is used to create expectations in others.* A good salesperson may describe a very quiet car as a little noisy so we are impressed on the test drive. A bad salesperson will over-promise, describing it as completely silent, which will set up a disappoint-ment upon driving.

**8.  *The advantages of deception must be balanced against its impact on credibility*.** A salesperson who says a very quiet car is a little noisy increases their credibility by demonstrating a higher standard for truth.

**9.  *All opinions are eventually measured against outcomes*.** The most successful car salespeople in the world are those who care more about a long-term relationship than an immediate sale.

## 2.1.4 Surprise

Sun Tzu's five key methods on the creation of surprise depends on the nature of information.

*"It is the same in all battles.*
*You use a direct approach to engage the enemy.*
*You use surprise to win."*
Sun Tzu's The Art of War 5:2:1-3

*"A true leader always keeps an element of surprise up his sleeve, which others cannot grasp but which keeps his public excited and breathless."*
Charles de Gaulle

**General Principle:** Information can be used to create surprise.

## Situation:

We are continuously bathed in a flood of new information, and yet little of this new information really surprises us. Our news comes from a worldwide network. Few of the events that affects our lives directly on a day-to-day basis are covered by the news. Like viewers of a television show, we think of ourselves as merely spectators, the audience, of the news. This is a dangerous and destructive attitude toward information. It distances us psychologically from the flow of information that Sun Tzu teaches is the key to our success. One problem is that too much of our information network lies outside of our competitive neighborhood where events do impact our lives. Another is that, despite the constant flow of events, we start to expect that our lives will continue much as before. This expectation sets us up for the surprise that completely undermines our position.

## Opportunity:

Innovation is the attacker's advantage. Sun Tzu's strategy leverages innovation, identifying people's expectations and using those expectations as the basis for creating surprise. We must see ourselves as the actors not merely the audience. When we generate new possibilities, others must adjust to us and we have to worry less about adjusting to them. Our goal is simply to make consistently better decisions that those around us. Sun Tzu's strategy is about improving our chances over time. The more we use surprise and the less we are victims of it, the more successful we will be. Moves to a new position are best completed by using surprise (7.0 Creating Momentum). In both cases, we must know how the nature of information creates the expectations that makes surprise possible.

## Key Methods:

These are Sun Tzu's five key methods describing the role information in creating surprise.

*1. Surprise is only possible because events violate expectations*. We are surprised because things don't happen as we expect. We use information to create expectations. Innovation is continuous, but people are largely blind to change. Surprise is sudden, discontinuous intrusion of an innovation in a situation. Innovation is unexpected because it is unpredictable. But, of course, it is not unpredictable if we are the ones doing the innovating. Surprise is how we use expectations (2.1.3 Strategic Deception).

*2. The expectations needed to create surprise can be either unthinking or realistic*. We can sometimes use unthinking expectations to catch people when they are unaware, but the consistent use of surprise requires intentionally creating realistic expectations (7.2.2 Preparing Expectations).

*3. Unthinking expectations can be used to create surprise when people lose contact with their environment*. We are doing something, but our attention is elsewhere. Since strategy is all about adapting to the environment, the failure to pay attention to what is going on around us is always a mistake (1.4 The External Environment).

*4. Realistic expectations cannot be surprised when people respond in a commonplace way.* Realistic expectations arise form knowing standard methods. In studying Sun Tzu, we learn competition's "standard methods," which are the range of typical actions that usually take place in a given situation. Standard methods are proven practices. People usually take certain actions in a given situation because those actions work. Often those actions work because the situation itself was designed for those actions to work (7.2 Standards First).

*5. Realistic expectations can only be surprised by innovation.* Innovation is a new idea, a new method, often unproven. It is the complementary opposite of standard methods. Like all complementary opposites, standard methods and innovation form a single system. In this system, these seemingly opposite and opposing forces generate each other in a continuous cycle. Innovation creates a new set of possibilities, which eventually become the new standard. That new standard becomes the basis for future innovation. Standard methods and innovation continually recreate each other in an endless stream(7.1.3 Standards and Innovation).

## Illustration:

These ideas can be illustrated simply by thinking about driving a car.

*1. Surprise is only possible because events violate expectations.* As we drive down the road, the car ahead of us can go straight, turn right, or turn left. We don't know what it will do, but we are not surprised by any of these choices because we expect them.

*2. The expectations needed to create surprise can be either unthinking or realistic.* People can forget that they are driving and be surprised by a normal driving experience, but if we want to surprise drivers, it is best to create a situation that normally doesn't happen while they are driving.

*3. Unthinking expectations can be used to create surprise when people lose contact with their environment.* The car ahead of us suddenly brakes. We are surprised. It is not that we didn't know cars could brake. We are surprised because we had temporarily forgotten that we were driving.

*4. Realistic expectations cannot be surprised when people respond in a commonplace way.* It is realistic to expect the car in front of us to turn right, turn left, go straight, speed up, or slow down. If we are paying attention, when it does any of these things, we should not be surprised. These possibilities are standard methods, representing the range of what is normal and predictable.

*5. Realistic expectations can only be surprised by innovation.* If the car in front of us suddenly floats into the sky or sinks into the earth, we would be surprised. This is not what is realistically expected. These are not standard methods for a car. If we have set up a trick where a car that is driving is suddenly is lifted off the road by crane, people will be surprised.

## 2.2 Information Gathering

Sun Tzu five key methods on gathering competitive information.

*"...bureaucrats worship the value of their salary money too dearly.*
*They remain ignorant of the enemy's condition.*
*The result is cruel."*

Sun Tzu's The Art of War 13:1:12-14

*"When action grows unprofitable, gather information; when information grows unprofitable, sleep."*

Ursula K. LeGuin

**General Principle:** How we gather information determines how we see our positions.

## Situation:

Sun Tzu puts the value of information higher than that of money. In most forms of competition, our definition of "winning" is far from obvious. It depends on what we consider valuable. Mistakes are even made confusing the most universal measures: money, time, and information. Our gathering of information starts with developing a broader perspective about what knowledge is the key to our success. The information that we gather shapes our very understanding of success. A limited perspective loses sight of both the broad possibilities and strict limitations of what is possible. When we do not see the possibilities, we miss finding a way to advance our position in unexpected ways. When we do not see the limitations, we make costly mistakes.

## Opportunity:

Competition is based upon the idea of comparing positions (1.3.1 Competitive Comparison). The comparison is based only on the information that we gather. Before we can know how to compare positions, we must understand how our information affects our perception of positions. We gain our advantage by knowing what types of information are most important in comparing positions and identifying success. Success becomes easier when we understand all the dimensions in which it can be attained. The information that we gather defines and shapes our understanding of success.

## Key Methods:

We must keep the following four key methods in mind when we gather strategic information.

*1. Information gathering depends on our interactive relationships with other people*. Competition is a human endeavor, dependent on subjective impressions as well as objective fact. Though there is an infinite amount of information available from impersonal sources such as the Internet, very little of that information is valuable for building our strategic perspective. In building a network, we have to think about two aspects of information: its quantity and its quality (2.2.1 Personal Relationships).

*2. To know what information to gather, we need proven mental models*. It is always easier and faster to use templates for gathering information. In a competitive situation, we do not have time to work through all the complexities of a situation. We cannot measure or analyze all potentially meaningful details in a give situation or position since many are unique. However, we can quickly work through mental models, comparing our current situation an existing model to identify key information. Sun Tzu's system is a generic model (2.2.2 Mental Models).

**3. *The five element model provides a universal template for gathering key information*.** The five elements provide a starting point for all information gathering. We must understand how the key aspects of mission, climate, ground, command, and methods generally determine position. Mastering this model assures that we don't miss key aspects that are important in all such comparisons (1.3 Elemental Analysis).

**4. *Every competitive field has its own "rules of the ground" for specialized information gathering*.** Sun Tzu's principles are generic, meta-rules, applying to every type of competitive comparison. Each competitive field also has its own, specialized measures for success. The rules of the ground can depend solely on people and their opinions. Other times, those rules are dictated by the physical constraints of the competitive environment. There are arbitrary rules and fixed rules. There are conditional principles and universal principles. (8.3 Securing Rewards).

**5. *We need a common vocabulary for information gathering*.** This allows us to communicate the key strategic issues more quickly. Much of this vocabulary may be unique to our competitive arena, but Sun Tzu's system provides a common vocabulary for discussing competitive issues more broadly (2.2.3 Standard Terminology).

## Illustration:

Let us quickly apply these key methods to understand how information gathering works for a small business owner.

**1. Information gathering depends on our interactive relationships with other people.** The key competitive information that we need comes from talking to other business people, other people in our industry, our customers, our suppliers, and other such sources.

**2. To know what information to gather, we need proven mental models.** We will get a lot of information almost randomly as we talk to people. A customer will mention a product. Another business in our area will mention an accountant. Someone else will discuss a problem with employee taxes. We cannot keep track of these different pieces of information unless we have a mental model that organizes and prioritizes them. Those models also guide us to ask the right questions.

**3. The five element model provides a universal template for gathering key information.** Sun Tzu teaches us to identify the goals of those with whom we are working, recognize issues of business climate, learn aspects of the ground, parse people's character, and seek specific methods.

**4. Every competitive field has its own "rules of the ground" for specialized information gathering.** Consider what "winning" means for a business. The same business can be compared to its competition in many different dimensions. One business can be more successful than its competitors in market share. Another can be more successful in profitability. A third can be more successful in total growth. Another can be more successful in percentage of growth. Still another can be measure customer satisfaction in repeat business.

**5. We need a common vocabulary for information gathering.** Business accounting has its language. Various industries have their own more specific language. Sun Tzu's offers a standard for more generic communication.

## 2.2.1 Personal Relationships

Sun Tzu's five key methods on why information depends on personal relationships.

*"You don't have local guides?*
*You won't get any of the benefits of the terrain."*
Sun Tzu's The Art of War 11:7:5-6

*"Personal relationships are the fertile soil from which*
*all advancement, all success, all achievement in real life*
*grows."*

Ben Stein

**General Principle:**  Only interactive personal relationships can discover quality information.

## Situation:

Sun Tzu taught that success depends on the quality of our information and that our information depends solely on our personal relationships. In understanding our situation, we don't know what we need to know. Literally. From our limited perspective, we have blind spots when it comes to our situations. We cannot describe where those blind spots are and what we are missing because we don't know. The most basic challenge in developing a contact network goes back to the problem of information quantity versus quality. More contacts do not necessarily mean more complete information. In developing a contact network, we can only stay productively in touch with a limited number of people. Contact networks have limits. It takes time and effort to maintain the relationships upon which a contact network is built. If we grow our contact network beyond that limit, that network actually produces less useful information than a smaller network.

## Opportunity:

For Sun Tzu, strategy is about making unique connections. In this regard, human relationships are uniquely powerful. The most powerful force in the world is people caring for other people. When others care about us, even a little, they turn the wonderful power of the human mind to our situation. When we care about others, we will move mountains for them. In looking for a needle in a haystack, more information doesn't help. It is just bringing in more hay. Our relationships harness the processing power of the human mind. Each of us has our own mental powers. Putting together a contact network is only partly about having people with right range of information. (2.4 Contact Networks). It depends heavily upon having the right human connections with the people involved.

# Key Methods:

Personal relationship are the key to good information because of the following five key methods.

*1. Our key information comes from our interactive personal relationships with other people.* Though there is an infinite amount of information available from impersonal, non-interactive sources, sources like the Internet, very little of that information is valuable for building strategic perspective. In building a network, we have to think about two aspects of information: its quantity and its quality. Quality information comes from personal connections with other people (2.4 Contact Networks).

*2. Our personal relationships harness the minds of others.* Only a human mind can filter through the flood of information for what might be valuable to a specific other person. Our relationships with others focus their minds on our unique situation. That focus is only possible within a relationship. Given that focus, they can fill in our spotty and limited perspective and help us see where our opportunities might lie (2.0 Developing Perspective).

3. *Personal relationships can identify important information that we didn't know was important.* A machine can only search for the information the we know that we need. In competitive environments, we often simply don't know the key information that we need. We rely upon our personal relationships to fill in our blind spots. Unlike machines, people can find valuable information for us that *we didn't know* we were looking for but only if they care to do so (1.2.3 Position Complexity).

*4. Personal relationships harness the power of caring about each others' goals.* When we make a connection, the connection point is our shared philosophy. Our caring is where our common mission lies. That shared mission can start with something as simple as filling in each others' blind spots ( 1.6.1 Shared Mission).

*5. There is an inverse relationship between the number of our personal relationships and their quality.* Some people have a greater capacity for personal relationships than others, but there is always a limit. Relationships take time. Like all resources, our time is limited. We can know a lot of people well enough to know if we can trust them. Too many different views from to many different people who we don't know how to trust, doesn't help us. As with information, more is not necessarily better (3.1.1 Resource Limitations).

## Illustration:

Let us look at all of these ideas from the perspective of people trying to their own small business and worried about government regulations.

*1. Our key information comes from our interactive personal relationships with other people.* Business people don't need to know everything as much as they need to know people who know what they need to know.

*2. Our personal relationships harness the minds of others.* There are hundreds of new laws under considerations with thousands of pages of text. Only someone who knows both the business person's industry and is experienced with the application of those laws is in a position to know about specific threats.

3. *Personal relationships can identify important information that we didn't know was important.* A business person who discovers new opportunities through its contacts focuses less on general news and more on the specifics of his or her situation. If that person has other contacts who have seen cycles of government activism come and go, he or she worries less about what cannot be controlled.

*4. Personal relationships harness the power of caring about each others' goals*. This is the basis of all "mastermind" type groups. The difference in Sun Tzu's strategy is that we try to take a more systematic approach to building a contact network. We use a more systematic approach because great contact networks do not just happen.

**5.  *There is an inverse relationship between the number of our personal relationships and their quality*.** In the deluge of information today, if small business people know too many people, they are bound to get lots of contradictory advice, which creates more of a problem than it solves.

# 2.2.2 Mental Models

Sun Tzu's five key methods on how mental models simplify decision-making.

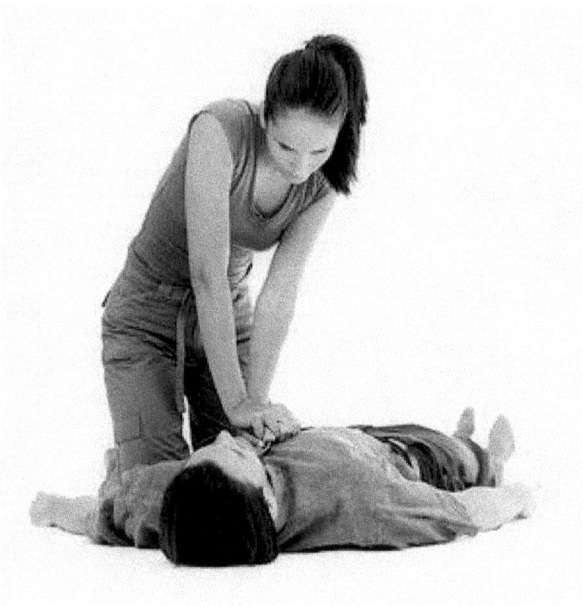

*"Military leaders must be experts in knowing how to adapt to find an advantage."*

Sun Tzu's The Art of War 8:1:14

*"Even people who are not geniuses can outthink the rest of mankind if they develop certain thinking habits."*

Charles Darwin

**General Principle:** Experts use mental models to quickly prioritize their responses to situations.

## Situation:

Sun Tzu's system converts information into decisions. On the front-lines of decision-making, new situations are constantly arising. Amateurs try to reason their way through these situations. Sun Tzu taught that experts compare ther current situation with a large, set of common situations and recurring conditions to choose the best course of action. As modern research always shows , experts are able to make the right decisions almost instantly from mental models. Given the complex dynamics of competitive environments, simply picking through the information and putting together a plan is virtually impossible. When we work through the problem analytically, quickly knowing the appropriate response seems impossible. The challenge is understanding how experts work their magic.

## Opportunity:

Sun Tzu's methods are best understood as a series of interconnected mental models.

Mental models describe common, generic situations and conditions that key us to make the right decision. To make good decisions, we compare our current situation with these mental models. It is always easier and faster to make comparisons than to figure things out. In a production environment, we have time to reason through situations. In a competitive environment, we do not have the luxury of time. Situations are too complex. We analyze all potentially meaningful details. We must quickly work through a list of mental models, comparing our current situation to these models, to quickly identify the appropriate response.

## Key Methods:

This methods of comparing current conditions to generic mental models is used throughout strategy to make instant decisions. This method is founded on some key methods for making good decisions under pressure.

*1. Sophisticated mental models describe a wide variety of common situations.* People can either build their mental model over years of practice or though intense periods of training (7.2.1 Proven Methods).

*2. Current situations are compared to mental models using a few key factors.* As new situations arise, those using mental models aren't distracted by every aspect of the situation. They only have to compare the situations to their mental models to identify the key aspects (1.3 Elemental Analysis).

*3. Mental models are first compared for situation identification.* While many mental models may touch upon aspects of a situation, a given situation will match one mental model most closely. This allows us to quickly orient ourselves(6.1 Situation Recognition).

*4. The situation is then compared to the mental model for any unexpected characteristics.* Once we have a template, we can easily see what doesn't fit. Every situations is unique, but if there are too many points of mismatch, we must ask if we are using the right model (1.8.2 The Adaptive Loop).

*5. The right model gives experts instant access to set of guidelines for making fast, good decisions.* While decisions must still be adapted to unique aspects of the situation, the mental model offers a reusable template for success. This is much faster than other forms of decision-making and more often comes to the correct decision. (5.3 Reaction Time).

## Illustration:

While this same process is used for making every decision in a front-line environment, perhaps the decisions of medical experts best illustrate how it works. In this illustration, we compare medical decision making with making any strategic decision.

*1. Sophisticated mental models can describe a wide variety of common situations.* Medical professionals are taught mental models as the key symptoms of a large number of specific medical conditions. Strategy professions are taught the key elements of a large number of specific strategic situations.

*2. Current situations are compared to mental models using a few key factors*. Medical professionals quickly check through the key areas of symptoms checking blood pressure, iris response, body temperature, etc. Strategy professions work through key aspects of position, mission, climate, ground, etc.

*3. Mental models are first compared for situation identification*. Medical professionals quickly connect a given symptom with the highest probability problem, for example, a high temperature with infection. Strategy professionals do the same, for example, connecting a lack of mission with a lack of unity and focus.

*4. The situation is then compared to the mental model for any unexpected characteristics*. Medical professionals then test to confirm the diagnosis, for example, confirming an infection by a blood test. Similarly, strategic professionals test for a lack of unity by probing alliances for potential defectors. If these tests prove negative, medical professional go back to looking for more key symptoms.

*5. The right model gives experts instant access to set of guidelines for making fast, good decisions*. If the diagnosis is confirmed, the standard treatments are used, i.e., antibiotics for infection or the use of division on disunity.

## 2.2.3 Standard Terminology

Sun Tzu five key methods regarding how mental models must be shared to enable communication.

*"This is the art of war:*
*1. Discuss the distances.*
*2. Discuss your numbers.*
*3. Discuss your calculations.*
*4. Discuss your decisions.*
*5. Discuss victory."*

Sun Tzu's The Art of War 4:4:4-10

*"Philosophy is written in that great book which ever lies before our eyes.We cannot understand it if we do not first learn the language and grasp the symbols in which it is written."*

Galileo Galilei

**General Principle:** Shared mental models improve communication by giving us a common language.

## Situation:

Communication is based upon a shared understanding of how the world works. The problem is that most of us have no shared vocabulary for dealing with the concepts that Sun Tzu teaches. In some cases, the words fit the ideas poorly. For example, we see "competition" as "conflict" not "comparison." For other concepts, such as complementary opposites , we have no words. We have been all been trained to talked about problem solving in the terms of linear or industrial thinking. While we learned about Sun Tzu's strategy from our life experiences, people lack common terms even if they have learned similar lessons. Without a common conceptual framework and vocabulary, we have to work a lot harder in gathering information to develop our strategic perspective.

## Opportunity:

Given a common conceptual framework and vocabulary, not only can we communicate the key strategic issues more quickly, but we can develop a powerful, shared perspective for identifying opportunities for each other. Our education may work against us, but our experience works for us. We all subconsciously recognize that step-by-step planning is only half the solution. The other half is our ability to instantly adapt to changes in environment. When we share this concept with our contact network, everyone in the network benefits and the quality of our strategic perspective improves dramatically.

## Key Methods:

*1. We must work with others to develop a common language for discussion competitive situations.* The mental models used in Sun Tzu's strategy were designed to facilitate this process. The process of developing a common language regarding external strategy isn't difficult, but it demands a effort. Information gathering doesn't stop with the right range of personal relationships (2.2 Information Gathering).

**2. Standard terminology can eliminate the confusion between *external challenges* and *internal control*.** The value of information gathering is in its external focus. As special terminology can maintain that focus. While everyone has opinions about how others could better manage the controlled areas of their lives, our contact networks are more effective in helping us developed perspective on our environment (1.9 Competition and Production).

**3. Standard terminology starts with the terms of elemental positioning.** This means specifically covering all five aspects of a position-- mission, climate, ground, leaders, and methods. This assures us more complete information and a more complete perspective (1.3 Elemental Analysis).

**4. The use of standard terminology gradually educate others in the models of Sun Tzu's strategy.** Mental models are based in a certain description of reality. One of the Institute's missions here is to develop a standard vocabulary for discussing strategic situations based on the standards developed by Sun Tzu (2.2.2 Mental Models , 7.2 Strategic Standards).

**5. Terminology models rely less on details such as specific measurements and more on relative comparisons.** Our minds cannot keep track of too much detail. Relative comparisons are easier to visualize and remember, especially when limited to the five key elements (1.3.1 Competitive Comparison).

**6. Terminology models restrict us to discussions of real alternatives.** It is easy and seductive to compare elements of positions against imaginary ideals, but positioning takes place in the real world, among real alternatives. Nobody and nothing are perfect. The idea of perfection, especially thinking anything or anyone is perfect, is a form of self-deception. The more we restrict ourselves to real situations, the more useful a common vocabulary becomes (2.1.3 Strategic Deception).

## Illustration:

Let us illustrate these principles in terms of our romantic relationships, especially in terms of identifying romantic opportunities within a community of people.

*1. We must work with others to develop a common language for discussion competitive situations.* No one really has a concrete language for discussing their position in relationships. Sun Tzu can help.

*2. Standard terminology can eliminate the confusion between <u>external challenges</u> and <u>internal control</u>.* While people love to gossip about the intimate details of other people's relationships, these are the areas where information is the very poorest. Information about the externals, i.e., who is going where with whom doing what is much more reliable and useful.

*3. Standard terminology starts with the terms of elemental positioning.* Relationships like all positions depend on a shared mission (philosophy and goals), the dynamics of climate (changes such as aging), ground (especially economics), leadership (matters of character or, so often, its lack or excesses), and methods (what people like to do in relationships).

*4. The use of standard terminology gradually educate others in the models of Sun Tzu's strategy.* We can be frustrated by a situation, but it helps a lot to know which of the nine common situations it represents. We can respond appropriately to a serious situation in a relationship differently than a difficult situation only if we understand the real distinctions between them. (Serious situations require more resources while difficult ones require persistence.)

*5. Terminology models rely less on details such as specific measurements and more on relative comparisons.* While physical dimensions (height, weight, etc.) are easily quantified, the most important characteristics defining people in relationships are not. Both types of characteristics make more sense in comparisons: Joe is taller than Jim. Jane is more outgoing that Jill.

6. ***Terminology models restrict us to discussions of real alter-natives.*** Perfect relationships are imaginary and imaginary relationships are for imaginary people. The tendency to compare people with idealized, imaginary versions in the media is very destructive to all relationships.

# 2.3 Personal Interactions

Sun Tzu's six key methods on making progress through personal interactions.

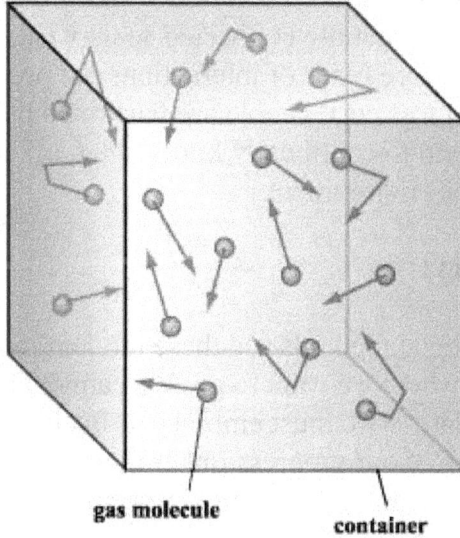

gas molecule        container

*"Internal and external events force people to move."*
Sun Tzu's The Art of War 13:1:6

*"History is the record of an encounter between character and circumstances."*
Donald Creighton

**General Principle:** We only advance our position through our interactions with other people.

## Situation:

In a competitive environment, plans constantly collide resulting in situations that no one plans. The encounters are like molecules of gas bumping off of each other. As a gas is heated, its molecules become more energetic, bouncing off of each other more frequently. The same is true of positions in a competitive environment. As we put energy into our moves, our contacts with others becomes more and more frequent. In a more connected society (see Networked World), more and more types of interactions are possible over greater distance at less cost. People are frustrated because all these random events seem to continually knock them off course, but that is the nature of the environment.

## Opportunity:

Sun Tzu's strategic methods use these random interactions with others to take us where we want to go. We cannot change the nature of our environment, so we must embrace it. Each interaction must become the source of our progress rather than an obstacle. The path in this environment cannot be planned. Each interaction will take us in a new direction, but if we know how to navigate this environment, the sum of all these changes takes us to our goals. Sun Tzu's strategy is not a game of solitaire. It is always played with, among, and off of other people. It is not about what we do alone. It is about how others react to what we do and how we react to their reactions.

## Key Methods:

Perhaps half the concepts in Sun Tzu's work deal with the key methods regarding the predictable and unpredictable parts of human interactions, but the following six key methods are critical to having the right perspective.

*1. Sun Tzu's methods utilize our interactions with others to advance our positions*. In life, we can never move directly toward our goals. We only get to our goals by "bouncing" off of other people in our interactions with them. Sun Tzu's strategy isn't, as people often mistakenly think, simply a contest of "beating" opponents. It is about advancing positions which requires us to interact with others (1.1 Position Paths).

**2. We can only execute our decisions by interacting with others.** We do not compete on a deserted island. The methods of adaptive strategy is designed to work solely within the confines of human interaction. In terms of more economic, professional, personal, and social goals, advancing our position usually means winning the acceptance and support of others. We describe the process of positioning as building up our position so that others cannot attack it and ideally want to join. Our position is our rank, status, station, and standing formed from people's attitudes, views, opinions, and perceptions about us (1.5.2. Group Methods).

**3. These interactions create a game of discovery.** We discover our possibilities through our interactions with others. Others discover possibilities in their interactions with us. We do not approach interaction with the goal of controlling people. We approach interactions with a sense of unknown potential. We can only find our path to our goals through those interactions. Our path to our goals can dramatically change from these interactions (2.3.1 Action and Reaction).

**4. Each interaction we have is compared with all other interactions.** In every form of competition, our positions are always evaluated by comparison with other positions. Both we and the people with whom we interact are constantly doing these evaluations. This creates a highly interactive environment where each interaction creates expectations for future interactions (1.3.1 Competitive Comparison).

**5. We must consciously work _not_ to get ahead of ourselves in our interactions.** This is one of the basic reasons why adaptive strategy isn't a form of planning. While we can look ahead, we must always decide and react to the here and now. Yes, we try to out-think other people, but that starts by thinking on our feet, during our interactions. When we get ahead of ourselves, we make assumptions about what other people will or will not do. Those assumptions are almost always wrong. People often know how they are going to react beforehand so we cannot as well. (2.3.2 Reaction Unpredictability).

6. ***Key information that we know we need comes only from our personal interactions.*** Sun Tzu's strategy teaches us the key elements of information. We need the help of others to get that information from vast quantities of information in the environment. Every contact is an opportunity for gathering that key information. The really valuable information is usually what is locked up inside of other people's heads (2.2.1 Personal Relationships).

## Illustration:

The phone rings. An email arrives. It is a new contact. We don't know who this person is or whether or not the contact offers us an opportunity.

1. ***Sun Tzu's methods utilize our interactions with others to advance our positions.*** Only through our contacts with others can we change their perception of our position. 99% of the emails we get may be meaningless in terms of our position, but that remaining 1% is critical to it.

2. ***We can only execute our decisions by interacting with others.*** In the end, our efforts must affect others or they affect no on. The most brilliant sales pitch, the most wonderful product, the most brilliant idea have no affect on the world until they touch the lives of others.

3. ***These interactions create a game of discovery.*** If we see the contact as an interruption, we will miss any opportunity that it might offer. Often, it will offer no opportunity, but we will never discover new opportunities if we assume every contact is a waste of our time.

4. ***Each interaction we have is compared with all other interactions.*** A person contacting us probably has very low expectations. That makes it easy for us to exceed those expectations by responding in a more positive way than they expect.

**5. *We must consciously work <u>not</u> to get ahead of ourselves*.** We must listen first and gauge where the person making contact is come from and respond in a way that itsn't so far outside their expectations that our response seemed inappropriate.

**6. *Key information that we know we need comes only from our personal interactions*.** Even if the contact offers no other opportunities long term, it is always an opportunity for gathering information about how others see our positions and why they are contacting us.

# 2.3.1 Action and Reaction

Sun Tzu's eight key methods on how we advance based on how others reaction to our actions.

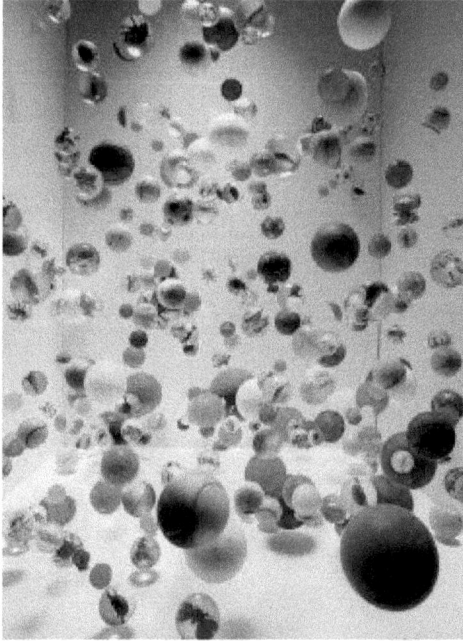

*"You must force the enemy to move to your advantage.*
*Use your position.*
*The enemy must follow you."*
                                        Sun Tzu's The Art of War 5:4:16-18

*"To every action there is an equal and opposite reaction."*
                                        Sir Isaac Newton

**General Principle:** Our decisions about action must factor in the opposing reactions of others over multiple encounters.

## Situation:

Good competitive decision-making seems convoluted to those who don't understand it. In a competitive environment , we cannot simply go in a straight line toward our goals. Instead, we reach our goals only through bouncing off of other people. When we want a specific reaction from someone, we often get the opposite. The more we push, the harder they push back. This is known in psychology as reactance. Each interaction changes our direction in some small way, putting both parties on a slightly different path. Each interaction take us both in a new direction. As others affect us, we also affect them. This is only a problem if we are trapped in the industrial mindset of linear thinking.

## Opportunity:

When we developed the adaptive mind of a warrior, we can enjoy the uncertainties of interaction. It keeps life interesting. It makes it more of a challenge. Sun Tzu's strategy is sometimes a matter of anticipating the moves of others. Other times, it is realizing that there are opportunities in human interactions that we cannot anticipate. In our most important interactions, we don't bounce off of each other just once. We bounce off of each other again and again. Each iteration is an opportunity for learning on both sides. We learn about others and they learn about us. Knowledge gained from past interactions is factored into future ones.

## Key Methods:

The following eight key methods describe how Sun Tzu sees the reactive nature of relationships.

*1. Our actions must consider how people are free to react and what their freedom will mean to future interactions.* While we sometimes describe strategy as out-thinking our opponents, it is more accurate to say that we want to include others and their freedom to act within our thinking. The competitive environment is defined by the interaction of people free to make their own decisions (1.4 The External Environment).

*2. In a competitive environment, reactions to our actions are unpredictable.* We can never count on others doing what we assume they will do. We cannot assume that they do what they say. We cannot even assume that they will do what is in their best interests, though that is a safer bet. Often, people don't know what they will do until the moment they act (2.3.2 Reaction Unpredictability).

*3. It is always easier to predict negative reactions than positive ones to our actions.* If we push people, we can be fairly certain that they will push back. From this fact we get the value of negative psychology. Sometimes it is easier to get people to do what we want if we pretend that we don't want it (6.8 Competitive Psychology).

4. *A single interaction makes it easier to set up future interactions.* While the chance that we encounter any given individual are small, the chances that we encounter someone again after encountering them once are much greater, especially if that is our goal (1.8.2 The Adaptive Loop).

*5. Multiple interactions are much easier to guide than a single interaction*. Over multiple reactions, we build up trust and certain expectations. While we can have some influence over a single reaction, the influence of both parties grows over the course of a relationship (1.8.4 A Probabilistic Process).

*6. We seek multiple interactions that take us mutually in the direction of our different desires*. Our bounces off of other people are guided. While we compete with one another in how we are compared, we can often work together to make faster progress toward our goals. This means that we can consider where each bounce takes us not only individually but as a group. The best relationships are those where the process of continually bouncing off of each other takes us where we both want to go. Organizations develop their external strength from the shared mission of their internal interactions. We bounce off each other within an organization so that as a group we make better progress in our shared external environment (1.6.1 Shared Mission).

*7. One big positive interaction can make up from a lot of costly little interactions.* This dynamic of mutual progress is not as simple as the concept of "win/win" suggests. The unspoken assumption in win/win is that each party gets something out of every single interaction. In real life, our interactions are seldom so simple. We are bouncing around, not going in a straight line. Even if the relationship is productive as a whole, many individual interactions are more costly than they are beneficial. However, one big positive bounce from a relationship can make up from a lot of little costly bounces (1.8.4 Probabilistic Process).

*8. We can learn people's unique character from their reactions to our actions.* Every person is unique. This means that we need quality information about other people's character, habits, and attitudes. When we know that we are going to be running into a person (or the same people again and again), we have to take the responsibility for trying to figure out how they "bounce" in their interactions with others. This requires us to join our understanding of character (1.5.1 Command Leadership).

## Illustration:

Let us illustrate these principles using one of our favorite topics, making sales.

*1. Our actions must consider how people are free to react and what their freedom will mean to future interactions.* In sales, we must accept that a sales encounter can go many different directions and that we cannot control that direction.

*2. In a competitive environment, reactions to our actions are unpredictable.* In sales, we should act as if we expect agreement, but we must be prepared for many other options as well.

*3. It is always easier to predict negative reactions than positive ones to our actions.* If we focus simply on getting the order, almost all of our interactions will be negative.

**4. A single interaction makes it easier to set up future interactions.** Asking questions in the sale qualification stage (the "Listen" phase of Sun Tzu's Progress Cycle) makes it easier to know what aspects of the product proposal to offer in the sales presentation stage (the "Aim" phase of Progress cylce).

**5. Multiple interactions are much easier to guide than a single interaction**. It is infinitely easier to get an agreement to future sales discussions than it is to get an agreement to an order after one discussion.

**6. We seek multiple interactions that take us mutually in the direction of our different desires**. Over many discussions, both the salesperson and the buyer have an opportunity to learn from interaction.

**7. One big positive interaction can make up from a lot of costly little interactions**. Over multiple interactions, salespeople have an opportunity to create the grounds for a mutually desirable agreement.

**8. We can learn people's unique character from their reactions to our actions**. Every person is unique. Continued sales relationships are built both upon both finding mutual goals and the pleasures of contact.

## 2.3.2 Reaction Unpredictability

Sun Tzu's seven key methods explaining why we can never exactly predict the reactions of others.

*"Surprise and direct action give birth to each other."*
*They are like a circle without end."*
Sun Tzu's The Art of War 3:2:24-25

*"It's all about exploring the more unpredictable aspects*
*in the character, not just fighting people."*
Victoria Pratt

**General Principle:** People's reactions can never be predicted exactly because every situation is unique and people creative.

## Situation:

The challenge in our interactions with others is predicting their likely reactions. This problem goes back to the difference between planning and strategy. In a internal, controlled environment, people are all working together and therefore try to keep each other informed about plans. In external, interactive environments, people are pursuing their own goals. People are free to do what they see as best. We cannot exactly predict their reactions because we cannot know their minds. That information is forever beyond our reach. People's reactions are not even completely rational. This is why Sun Tzu's strategy factors in a host of cognitive biases in people's reactions. Strategically, behaving predictably is dangerous. It can be just as dangerous to assume that we know what others will do.

## Opportunity:

Our opportunity is to respect people's freedom to act. Once we accept the idea of freedom, we realize that we must adapt. We then realize that we need to think in terms of probability rather than certainties. When we choose our actions based upon probabilities, we remain free ourselves. We are free to adjust to other possible reactions. We must gauge our actions based upon all the potential reactions of others. People are not machines. The competitive universe is not deterministic. It is filled with people just like us, who do not behave in an easily predictable manner. Since our individual choices depend on array of circumstances and values that others cannot know, we are constantly making surprising and novel choices. The same is true of everyone else as well.

# Key Methods:

The following seven key methods describe how Sun Tzu sees the unpredictable nature of reactions.

*1. People's reactions are unpredictable because our knowledge is limited.* While empathy is necessary for making good decisions, we must avoid risking too much on our assumptions. Our assumptions are based on how we would react to their situation. However we are not in their situation. Our perspective on their situation is different than their perspective. There are boundaries on what we can know (2.1.1 Information Limits).

*2. Reactions are unpredictable because we cannot know people's current priorities.* People's priorities change from moment to moment as different needs assert themselves over time. We cannot know for certain which needs will seem paramount to anyone at any given moment when a decision is made (1.6.3 Shifting Priorities).

*3. Reactions are unpredictable because we cannot know how people will react to change.* We cannot know what changes will capture people's attention nor how they will respond to those events. People often act out of habit but they only do so until they crave novelty. Every person feels the pressure of events in a different way (5.1.1 Event Pressure).

*4. Reactions are unpredictable because we cannot know how well others understand a situation.* Economics and game theory are based upon our acting rationally in our self-interest, but competitive environments are too complicated and chaotic for many people to discern where their interests lie. Since most people lack the mental models necessary put conditions into a larger context, their responses cannot be foreseen (2.2.2 Mental Models).

*5. Reactions are unpredictable because we cannot know all aspects of character.* This applies to both character flaws and strengths. It also applies to ourselves as well as others. Decisions arise at the intersection of knowledge and character. Knowing what to do isn't the same as having the courage or discipline to do it (1.5.1 Command Leadership).

**6. *Reactions are unpredictable because we cannot know what methods people use*.** We cannot even know exactly what skills people have or which skills they will apply to a given situation. People tend to use the methods to what they know best, even when those methods are poorly suited to the situation. Many keep their choice of methods a secret for very good strategic reasons. Others will simply try the first thing that pops into their head. Others will try to do things that they do not know how to do. Even when people use standard methods, they can change those methods to try and improve them (7.1.3 Standards and Innovation).

**7. *These uncertainties cannot be eliminated so they must be managed*.** We manage them in two ways. We learn the possible range of reactions (2.3.3 Range of Reactions) and we use a lot of questions (2.3.4 Using Questions).

## Illustration:

These limitations can be illustrated in every competitive arena.

**1. *People's reactions are unpredictable because our knowledge is limited*.** People enjoy watching sporting events because we can never know what is happening next.

**2. *Reactions are unpredictable because we cannot know people's current priorities*.** At the moment we contact someone, they may be so hungry that nothing else we do or say will make an impression.

**3. *Reactions are unpredictable because we cannot know how people will react to change*.** A change that seems exciting and attractive to us can seem frightening to someone else.

**4. *Reactions are unpredictable because w e cannot know how well others understand a situation*.** Think of all the alcoholics who insist that they don't have a problem.

**5. *Reactions are unpredictable because we cannot know all aspects of character*.** How often are people surprised by someone they trusted stabbing them in the back?

**6. *Reactions are unpredictable because we cannot know what methods people use*.** To a man with a hammer, everything looks like a nail. A fighter will tend to start swinging whenever they are in trouble even when each swing creates an opening.

7. ***These uncertainties cannot be eliminated so they must be managed.*** Smart sales people asked both open-ended questions that can go any direction and closed-ended questions that limit possible responses.

## 2.3.3 Likely Reactions

Seven key methods regarding the range of potential reactions in gathering information.

*"Another general fails to predict the enemy.*
*He pits his small forces against larger ones.*
*His weak forces attack stronger ones.*
*He fails to pick his fights correctly."*

Sun Tzu's The Art of War 10:2:27-30

*"The meeting of two personalities is like the contact of two chemical substances; if there is any reaction, both are transformed."*

Carl Gustav Jung

**General Principle:** Choose actions based upon the most likely responses.

## Situation:

Sun Tzu's methods depend on information, specifically our perspective on how people will react. While it is important to know that people's reactions are never certain, we must still predict others to succeed. Our challenge is identifying the situations in which reactions become relatively predictable. Competitive environments are defined by the fact that people are free to act and react how they desire. Our actions only produce their results through other people's reactions.

## Opportunity:

Competitive strategy is based on probabilities (1.8.4 A Probabilistic Process). Probabilities are based on situations and conditions. Though we cannot exactly predict what people will do in every situation, some situations are more predictable than others. While we cannot know every potential reaction of any given encounter, we can recognize specific situations in which people's reactions become more predictable. We play those probabilities, working to make sure that the unpredictable outcome of a single encounter does not determine our fate. In using Sun Tzu's strategic principles, each move is a small experiment. We never gamble everything on a single outcome because experiments fail more often than they succeed. However, through the repeated attempts of the adaptive loop, where we learn from each failure and adjust our methods, success becomes more and more likely over time (1.8.2 The Adaptive Loop).

## Key Methods:

We can know what people are most likely to do. We choose our actions based upon the range of most likely responses. In descending order of probability, people's general responses are :

*1. If they have responded to a similar situation in the past, people are likely to do what they have done in the past.* If people have chosen a given action before, they are likely to choose that action again. The more often they have chosen that action, the more likely they are to choose it again. However, at some point this behavior can switch to its opposite. However, usually something has to change in the environment for them to switch. People are creatures of habit. Developing new responses takes work. Unless we are given an incentive to change our responses, we will usually continue to do what we have been doing (1.1.1 Position Dynamics).

*2. At predicable spans of time, people's reactions are more likely to address certain cyclic physical needs.* These changes range from the daily cycles of hunger and the need for sleep to the annual cycles of the seasons to the long-term cycle of aging. People are the most predictable in terms of how and when they satisfy their physical needs (1.6.3 Shifting Priorities) and the demands of time ((1.4.1 Climate Shift).

*3. When faced with a threat or direct challenge, people are likely to react with the flight or fight response.* If people have very few strategic skills and little experience with a given situation, they are more likely to choose the flight and fight response. If we push people, they will either push back or flee. Which route they choose depends upon their character, but the greater the pressure on people who are untrained in situational probability, the more likely it is that they will choose one of these responses (Your Gut and Your Brain , 2.3.1 Action and Reaction).

*4. If people have made verbal commitments, they are more likely to react according to their commitments.* While people do lie in situations where it will give them an advantage, there are many more advantages in being seen as honest and trustworthy. When people commit to a course of action, they usually will follow that course of action, or at least try to do, what they said they will do. The value in getting verbal commitments is that is makes reactions more predictable (8.3.3 Rules of Engagement).

*5. When they fail to honor commitments, their most likely reaction is the opposite of what was promised.* When people break with commitments, they usually don't react a little differently than promised. They go the whole way. The commitments could have been an attempt to mislead, but they are also free to change their minds. However, they do not change their minds for slight adjustments. They do not change their minds unless the course they want to take is the reverse of what they promised (3.2.5 Dynamic Reversal).

*6. The more experience and trained people are in competition, their reactions are more likely to conform to Sun Tzu's principles.* Though most people are not trained in any systematic way in strategic decision-making, almost everyone discovers pieces of Sun Tzu's system through trial and error. As people learn a few of these principles and methods through experience, they will tend to apply them more broadly than they deserve, bringing us back to the first rule in this list. If we recognize patterns of response from someone, we can expect to see those same responses again, even when those responses are inappropriate to their situation. As Mark Twain said, "A cat that has sat on a hot stove won't sit on a hot stove again, or a cold one either." (6.0 Situation Response).

*7. People's reactions become more predictable if we can combine these elements.* People are more likely to do what they have said they will do if that is what they have done in the past. This is even more likely if their past actions fit into the flight and fight response. Which reaction they are likely to choose, depends on the specifics of their position: their motivation, the climate, the ground, their command, and their skills. Knowing people's motivations helps more than any other factor in understanding their potential choices. Knowing their skills and experience is the second most important factor (6.1.1 Conditioned Reflexes).

## Illustration:

Let us apply these key methods to predicting the reactions of a prospect confronted by a salesperson.

We can know what people are most likely to do. We choose our actions based upon the range of most likely responses. In descending order of probability, people's general responses are :

*1. If they have responded to a similar situation in the past, people are likely to do what they have done in the past.* The prospect's most likely response to a sales proposal is to continue their past patterns of buying or not buying over time.

*2. At predicable spans of time, people's reactions are more likely to address certain cyclic physical needs.* A salesperson can use the opportunity of a lunch invitation to change a prospect's past behavior. A smart salesperson will identify physical changes in the environment that should make the prospect reconsider his or her past decisions. Those decisions can never be wrong so conditions must change to set up the potential for a different purchasing decision.

*3. When faced with a threat or direct challenge, people are likely to react with the flight or fight response.* A salesperson cannot get a prospect out to lunch if the salesperson has put pressure on the prospect. The prospect will either flee or flight the pressure, making lunch with the salesperson an unattractive proposition.

*4. If people have made verbal commitments, they are more likely to react according to their commitments.* A smart salesperson gets a small commitment first. Instead of asking for a lunch meeting at the spur of the moment, he casually asks for a commitment to it at some future date. After getting that commitment, most people will follow through with it, even if they don't want to at the time.

*5. When they fail to honor commitments , their most likely reaction is the opposite of what was promised.* When the salesperson calls to confirm the promised lunch appointment, the prospect can simply say that he never made the commitment and that the salesperson is confused. The salesperson should be prepared for this possibility, being prepared to admit confusion and simply asked again.

*6. The more experienced and trained people are in competition, their reactions are more likely to conform to Sun Tzu's principles*. It takes time to learn the patterns of response from a prospect so that we can use them to our advantage. The entire system of action and reaction is designed to build positions over time rather than win orders on the first encounter.

*7. People's reactions become more predictable if we can combine these elements*. A salesperson should seek to develop repeated patterns, such are regular lunch dates with clients, learning how a given prospect typically reacts in a given situation.

## 2.3.4 Using Questions

Sun Tzus five key methods for using questions in gathering information and predicting reactions.

*"You must question the situation."*
Sun Tzu's The Art of War 1:2:2

*"To be able to ask a question clearly is two-thirds of the way to getting it answered."*
Carl Gustav Jung

**General Principle:** Questions are a powerful tool in working with others.

## Situation:

Sun Tzu's system of information gathering focuses on communication and leveraging people's reactions. We often keep our questions locked up in our head. We think of the questions that we have as internal. We fail to understand the value of getting those questions out of our head and communicating them with others. We avoid questions for a number of reasons. Often, we want to appear more knowledgeable than we really are. Even more often, we want avoid looking stupid. We are afraid of exposing our ignorance and therefore our vulnerabilities. When we ask a question, we are taking the risk of rejection. We sometimes prefer hearing ourselves talk rather than encouraging others to talk.

## Opportunity:

Good decisions depend on our ability to ask questions. We choose our actions to get the responses that we want from them. We cannot expect people to tell us what we need to know without our first telling them what we need to know. The use of questions is a powerful tool for predicting people's reactions. Asking questions actually controls people's minds, directing their attention where we desire. They are perhaps the most powerful tool in our arsenal of working with others through action and reaction.

## Key Methods:

The following key methods describe the use of questions in developing a strategy.

*1. Good methods continually leverage the power of questions.*
Questions both gather information and control the direction on an encounter. We cannot make decisions until we have an idea about

people's reactions to our actions. When we ask questions, people are forced to respond. Questions are a simple and powerful method to control other people's reactions to our actions (2.3.1 Action and Reaction).

**2. We can ask open-ended questions to solicit unknown information and potential reactions that we cannot foresee.** Our information is always incomplete. Our perspective is not that of others. The first and most valuable role of questions is harnessing other people's minds to help us fill in the blanks. As a result of our question and the thinking questions generates, many will offer alternatives that we could have never thought of on our own. Of course, we have to be open to hear these possibilities. These responses are extremely valuable, identifying new potential course of action working together (2.1.1 Information Limits).

**3. We can ask people directly about specific information and potential reactions to the suggested course of action.** We use these questions when we know what we want to know. A direct question gets people thinking. In many cases, people will not know what they will do. But by simply asking, we put them in a position where they have to think about their responses. Their initial reaction to the question is likely to be their initial reaction to the action. It is the least expensive test of an action (5.4.1 Value Tests).

**4. We can ask questions to shape people's reactions.** We cannot push people directly to do what we want. However, questions demand a response and to some degree, determine what actions people must consider. While there are principles about why peoples reactions **must** always have elements of unpredictability (2.3.2 Reaction Unpredictability) and other principles about the best ways to predict those reactions (2.3.3 Range of Reactions).

**5. If we cannot ask questions of someone directly, we can ask others who are close to them.** Information gathers in pools. While we want to get information, especially about people's plans, from the individuals involved, sometimes that isn't possible. In those cases, we need to go to those around them, those who have frequent contact with them. If we cannot contact those people, we can ask people who are in similar position. If we cannot do that, we can ask those who are more experienced in seeing similar people's reactions (8.4 Individual Contact).

## Illustration:

The obvious illustration here is in sales where asking questions is the heart of good method, but let us use the illustration of government decision-making because it also illustrates the most common problems in this area.

*1. Good methods continually leverage the power of questions.* We can see this mistake of failing to ask questions about people's reactions to government policy. Legislators treat the situations as static environments instead of a dynamic ones. For example, one of the biggest forces shaping economic decisions is the tax policy itself. but politicians routinely forecast tax revenue based upon economic activity before increased taxation without asking questions about how changes in taxes will change reactions. Forecasts about government policy, especially its costs, are always wrong because as a result of policy changes, people's activities change. We should ask people about how they would change their behavior in reaction to a new law instead of asking about how they feel about the intentions of such laws.

*2. We can ask open-ended questions to solicit unknown information and potential reactions that we cannot foresee.* We can ask people about their likely reactions to a new government policy. For example, if we plan to move to a given government health care proposal, we can ask about all the potential problems that they might foresee either in implementation of the proposed program or in people gaming the new system for personal benefit.

*3. We can ask people directly about specific information and potential reactions to the suggested course of action.* For example, if the government requires a small penalty for not getting medical insurance while forcing companies to provide insurance despite health problems, we should ask if people would wait to get insurance until they have a health condition that requires treatment.

*4. We can ask questions to shape people's reactions*. In asking questions about recent government policies, the tea party and similar movements have been able to galvanize large, popular movements seeking to redirect government.

5. *If we cannot ask questions of someone directly, we can ask others who are close to them.* If we don't trust the answers that people give us about health insurance, we can ask economists. We can ask people generally to their and others'. Given that health insurance cannot be denied on the basis of pre-existing conditions, most economists would predict that if the penalty is less expensive than insurance, people would simply wait until they develop health problems. Such programs must coerce people to buy insurance so that they cannot game the system by waiting to get sick. So coercing insurance companies to insure those with pre-existing conditions leads to more coercion, forcing everyone to buy insurance.

# 2.3.5 Infinite Loops

Four principles predicting reactions on the basis of the "you-know-that-I-know-that-you-know" problem.

*"They are like a circle without end.*
*You cannot exhaust all their possible combinations!"*
Sun Tzu's The Art of War 4:4:14

*"Our minds are finite, and yet even in these*
*circumstances of finitude we are surrounded by*
*possibilities that are infinite, and the purpose of life is to*
*grasp as much as we can out of that infinitude."*
John Ruskin

**General Principle:** Thinking about the reactions of others cannot be an infinite loop.

## Situation:

Before we act, we think about how others will react, but their reaction includes trying to foresee our reactions. There is a trap hidden in thinking about the cycles of action and reaction. It has no natural stopping point. As opponents plan, they naturally consider how we might do. So, in turn, before we act, we must consider not only how they will react but how they will think that we will react. They, in turn, know that we are thinking about what they are thinking about what we are thinking. In trying to find an advantage by thinking one step ahead of others, we find ourselves in an infinite loop of regression. Out-thinking others is not the same as out-positioning others.

## Opportunity:

Sun Tzu's methods require anticipating the moves of others. They also depend upon acting, quickly and decisively. The prejudice is toward action, since only action puts us back in touch with reality. The mental loops of thinking about what others are thinking about what we are thinking about their thinking trap us in a world of infinite imagination. Quick responses often work simply because others get bogged down in the infinite loop of possibilities. Time is our most valuable resource. We cannot lose sight of the fact that our opportunity in dealing with others. Our advantage is often as simple as making good decisions more quickly than most do.

## Key Methods:

The following five key methods describe how we handle the problem of over thinking a problem according to Sun Tzu's methods.

*1. We must recognize the "ad infinitum" decision loop of possibilities before we slide into it.* We cannot out-think our competition using a method of infinite regression and infinite possibilities while our lives, and especially the time we have for making a given decision, are extremely finite. Infinite loops consider more and more remote possibilities in each iteration. In a chess game, there are finite possibilities and only one goal. The number of potential actions and reactions in a game is large, larger than the number of atoms in the known universe, but they are still finite. In real life, there are infinite possibilities and infinite goals. The possibilities include moves that haven't even been invented yet but get invented because some enterprising individual sees new possibilities (1.8.3 Cycle Time).

*2. To escape infinite decision loops , we limit the number of elements considered in action and reaction cycles.* Every detail and direction can be entered into our calculations of what others will do if we let them. We do better if we limited our thinking to only the five key elements (1.3 Elemental Analysis). (2.3.1 Action and Reaction).

*3. To escape infinite decision loops, we limit thinking about action and reaction cycles to three or four iterations.* Experiments in human psychology and game theory show that almost everyone naturally looks ahead only two or three moves, so a single loop more is all we need to create a comparative advantage (1.3.1 Competitive Comparison).

*4. To escape infinite decision loops , we add additional iterations based directly on experience level.* Experienced people will tend to follow the principle above, which means we have to use four or five iterations. Of course, even more experienced people will use this rule as well. This give us the opportunity to see this entire lesson and infinite loop by referring to itself (2.3.5 Infinite Loops).

*5. To escape infinite decision loops , we **rely on actions rather than mental gymnastics**.* Imagination is a good and necessary part of competitive decision-making. However, it has a limit. At some point we must get real information and we can only get that from interaction not imagination. It is often better to ask others about potential cycles of actions and reactions rather than try to calculate these cycles alone. A crowd is better than the wisdom of any one person (2.3 Personal Interactions).

## Illustration:

The obvious illustration here is in sales where asking questions is the heart of good method, but let us use the illustration of government decision-making because it also illustrates the most common problems in this area.

*1. We must recognize the "ad infinitum" decision loop of possibilities before we slide into it.* In our seminars, we have an exercise that demonstrates the ad infinitum problem in decision-making. We tell everyone that the maximum potential prize is $100, but the actual prize amount depends on how much you bid. The prize will go to the person who bids the amount closest to 70% of the *average* bid in the group. This sets up the infinite loop because the winning bid is 70% of the average bid, but the average bid is based on people calculating 70% of the average bid. If everyone bid $100, the winning bid would be $70, but everyone knows that $70 is the maximum winning bid, so they should perhaps guess 70% of $70, which is $49. Of course, if everyone does that calculation, the winning bid would be 70% of $49 or $34.

*2. To escape infinite decision loops , we limit the number of elements considered in action and reaction cycles*. This is limited by the game itself to a single element: what will the average person guess. People have their mission, to win. They have a climate, limited time to decide. They have the ground rules of the game.This is a question of character and methods: what does the average person do.

*3. To escape infinite decision loops, we limit thinking about action and reaction cycles to three or four iterations*. We use this number because the average person makes between two and three loops, say 2.5 iterations. In this case, this means they would bid between $34 and $49 dollars (see above).

*4. To escape infinite decision loops , we add additional iterations based directly on experience level.* After running this exercise once, we can ask the same question again, after they have seen the right answer from the first iteration. They will be less that $34 because they learned from the outcome of the previous round.

5. *To escape infinite decision loops, we rely on actions rather than mental gymnastics.* While the game always has a winner, played enough times, the "right" answer is not playing at all because the right answer regresses to zero.

## 2.3.6 Promises and Threats

Sun Tzu's six key methods on the use of promises and threats as strategic moves.

*"You can make the enemy come to you.*
*Offer him an advantage.*
*You can give the enemy no advantage in coming to you.*
*Threaten him with danger."*
Sun Tzu's The Art of War 6:1:5-8

*"But as the arms-control scholar Thomas Schelling once noted, two things are very expensive in international life: promises when they succeed and threats when they fail."*
Don Piatt

**General Principle:** We should only make threats to deter actions and promises to impel actions.

## Situation:

Competition requires building up positions. This requires us to maximize our resources. In The Art of War, Sun Tzu constantly warns that we must judge people's intentions by their actions, especially when people communicate their commitment to future actions. We all communicate commitments in order to encourage people to act in a way that we desire today in order to get a reward or avoid a punishment tomorrow. The problem at the heart of any commitment is our believability. Making a threat or promise is easy, executing either commitment is costly. Making good on a threat requires punishing someone. Making good on a promise rewards someone. Both are costly to us.

## Opportunity:

Leveraging information is the least costly way to build up a position. The main alternative, making physical moves, is much more costly. Our opportunity is to leverage the inexpensive threat or the promise in a way that eliminates the more costly forms of effort (3.6 Leveraging Subjectivity). If a threat is believed, we reduce our costs because we never have to act on it. If a promise is trusted, the cost of honoring is less than the value we gain both in the current situation and future interactions.

## Key Methods:

The following six key methods describe the use of threats and promises from the perspective of Sun Tzu.

*1. We threaten to increase the perception of the costs of doing what we don't want.* Threats can help people avoid mutually destructive situations that would otherwise attract them. A threat would not be necessary if a move in a given situation did not potentially return benefits to one party at the expense of other (3.1.3 Conflict Cost).

*2. We promise to increase the rewards of doing what we desire.* Promises can help people achieve to mutually beneficial situations otherwise unavailable to them. A promise would not be necessary if a move was not more costly to one party that the other party. The reward balances the costs and rewards for both parties (3.1.2 Strategic Profitability).

**3. Both threats and promises depend totally on their communication and credibility.** Threats and promises must be heard and they must be believed. The most important aspect in being believed is our history. People judge our future behavior by our past behavior, or, as we say, our position is path with a history, not a disconnected point (1.1 Position Paths).

**4. In using threats and promises, others must believe that we are willing to sacrifice our future flexibility.** After the fact, executing a punishment or delivering a reward is going to be costly to us, so at that point in time, we would rather not do it. As Thomas Shelling wrote in **The Strategy of Conflic**t expresses, "The power to constrain an adversary depends upon the power to bind oneself." While these two ideas seem like opposites, they are actually two sides of the same coin (3.2.3 Complementary Opposites).

**5. Threats are better used for deterrence.** When successful, the undesirable action is deterred and the cost of extracting punishment is deferred. Threats designed to compel action encourage the minimum possible compliance and invite sabotage (2.3.1 Action and Reaction).

6. **Promises are better used to encourage an action.** When successful, the costs of the reward has already been "paid for" by the desired action. Promises designed to deter an action indefinitely require continuous payments for  uncertain future rewards (2.3.2 Reaction Unpredictability).

## Illustration:

Let us draw today's illustration from a little different competitive arena, parenting a teenager.

*1.  We threaten to increase the perception of the costs of doing what we don't want.* We threaten to "ground" a teenager if they do not honor their curfew.

*2.  We promise to increase the rewards of doing what we desire.* When we care more about getting A's than our teen does, we can promise are reward, such as extending driving privileges, for each "A's."

*3.  Both threats and promises depend totally on their communication and credibility.* The teen needs to know the curfew and the punishment and trust that we will actually enforce it.

*4.  In using threats and promises, others must believe that we are willing to sacrifice our future flexibility.* If the curfew is violated, we cannot suspend the grounding for "special events" or to relieve ourselves from constant nagging. If driving privileges are won by good grades, we must give up our own access to the vehicle during those times.

*5.  Threats are better used for deterrence.* The threat works to deter staying out as long as the teen desires.

*6.  Promises are better used to encourage an action.* The promise works to encourage more studying

## 2.4 Contact Networks

Five key methods regarding the range of contacts needed to create perspective.

> *"You need all five types of spies. No one must discover your methods.*
> *You will then be able to put together a true picture.*
> *This is the commander's most valuable resource."*
>
> Sun Tzu's The Art of War 13:2:7-11

> *"Networking is making links from people we know to people they know, in an organized way, for a specific purpose, while remaining committed to doing our part, expecting nothing in return."*
>
> Donna Fisher

**General Principle:** Contact networks gather information in the five key areas defining strategic situations.

## Situation:

No matter how well connected with think we are, the networks of contacts that we naturally develop in our lives are inherently limited. Natural contact networks are myopic, consisting of people who largely shared the same points of view. This occurs because we tend to keep in contact with people who are like ourselves. Our contacts tend to be the same age, have the same interests and opinions, live in the same areas, and, more and more often, work in the same industry if not company as we do. We cannot develop a broader perspective from talking to people who share the greater part of our perspective.

## Opportunity:

Sun Tzu based his design for information gathering around the five elements of a strategic position. We use the five elements our template for gathering information (1.3 Elemental Analysis). We need information about changing conditions (climate), our competitive arena (ground), those whose decisions affect our position (leader), the processes of the groups with whom we interact (methods), and the motivations guiding the people and groups who affect our position. Different types of people are better positioned to have these types information.

## Key Methods:

Note: In Sun Tzu's *The Art of War,* his term for information sources is traditionally translated into English as "spies," but the Chinese character was originally closer in meaning to the concept "conduits,""channels," or "go-between." In my book, *Nine Formulas for Business Success* , we update Sun Tzu's five types of spies to a nonmilitary setting, but keeping their alignment with the five key elements of a position. We describe the five key methods for the type of information conduits that we need.

*1. Old pros are people with experience in a specific competitive arena*. They know the rules of the **ground** and the implications of those rules. There is no more important teacher than experience on the ground (2.4.1 Ground Perspective).

*2. Fresh eyes only belong to those who see the changes in **climate** from a fresh perspective*. As people get older, they develop a more fixed perspective and a point of view. We all need to connect our perspective to those who see things from the perspective of the next generation (2.4.2 Climate Perspective).

*3. Insiders are those who know decision-makers whose decisions affect us*. If we are a salesperson, these are people who know our customers and how they think. If we are an employee, these are those who know our boss. Only people who are close to those whose decisions affect us can give us insight into their character (2.4.3 Command Perspective).

4. *Methods observers are people who can compare and contrast how we and our rivals operate.* These contacts can tell us about the best practices used by our competitors. We must learn and understand competitive practices to understand our position(2.4.4 Methods Perspective).

5. *Missionaries are those who carry our vision to others.* This last group shares our sense of value with the world. They have a real interest in your shared mission (2.4.5 Mission Perspective).

## Illustration:

These three types of people are needed in every contact network, whether we are talking about our business or our personal relationships. For our illustration, let us use the example of a person who is opening a small business. If we think that we want to open a new restaurant, what should our contact network look like?

*1. Old pros are people with experience in a specific competitive arena*. Before opening a new restaurant, we should definitely be talking to people with a lot of experience not only in running existing restaurants, but opening new ones. However, since this is the area of "ground," we should also be talking to people who know the specific location or area in which we are thinking of opening a restaurant.

*2. Fresh eyes only belong to those who see the changes in <u>climate</u> from a fresh perspective*. No matter what type of restaurant, we are opening, we want people to see it as new and exciting. This means we need to get in contact with young people, especially those who eat the kind of food we are thinking about offering to see what they find new and interesting in a restaurant.

*3. Insiders are those who know decision-makers whose decisions affect us*. In the restaurant, this category would include the food critics for the local paper, for popular blogs, and others who are in contact with your potential customers, perhaps even other businesses in the area you are working.

*4. Methods observers are people who can compare and contrast how we and our rivals operate*. These people are those who know restaurant operations, and it would include people who supply the restaurant business with equipment.

*5. Missionaries are those who carry our vision to others*. These people can be from any of the above categories, but who buy into the mission of our particular vision for a restaurant.

# 2.4.1 Ground Perspective

Sun Tzu's three key methods about getting information on a new competitive arena.

*"You need local spies."*

Sun Tzu's The Art of War 13:2:2

*"Experience is the best teacher, but a fool will learn from no other." Benjamin Franklin*

**General Principle:** Find old pros to learn the unique rules to the new competitive arena.

## Situation:

Each competitive arena is unique. It has its own form and shape. We call the component of competition with form and shape "the ground." Most conditions affecting our strategic decisions are ground conditions. Unfortunately, our instincts and our egos combine to make seeking out local guides to the ground harder than it should be. We are naturally more comfortable with people who share our level of knowledge about the ground. If we are new to a competitive arena, we connect most easily with other new people. The problem is that those people cannot help us. Most people are deluded about the depth of their knowledge. We are shy about connecting with those a lot more successful.

## Opportunity:

Sun Tzu's strategy teaches us how to organize ground characteristics into a meaningful picture (2.5 The Big Picture), but our contact network provides the pieces of information that we need to build that picture. Since our time is limited, we need to find the best and most comprehensive information as quickly as possible (3.1.6 Time Limitations). Our opportunity is making contact with the "old pros," who really know the territory. This is made easier because these old pros are too often overlooked today because youth is valued over experienced. When we seek out relationships with older people, we demonstrate that we value their experience. We make a positive impression when we do this because most older people would love the opportunity to pass on what they know.

## Key Methods:

It is easy to find old pros who can act as mentors because they are easy to identify. They stand out in a crowd because they are older. However, to build the best contact network, we need to remember the following key methods.

*1. **The best source of perspective on the new competitive arena are those who have a track record of success in that arena**. Actions speak louder than words. Most people learn the rules of the ground through painful trial and error, but a minority learn to avoid the errors more quickly than others. These people have demonstrated the ability to translate their knowledge into mental models (2.2.2 Mental Models).

*2. **The next best source of perspective on the new competitive arena are those who know a lot of other people in an area**. Some people are natural connectors, who are great at naturally developing contact networks. These people are especially good sources of connection with others. Most of what happens in our competitive neighborhood never makes it into the official media, and, when they do, rumors pass information about the interesting developments long before it appears even on the web (2.4 Contact Networks).

*3. **The next best source of perspective on the new competitive arena are those who have a long tenure**. Survival in an area demonstrates a level of competence and there is no more important teacher in life than experience. The longer people survive in a given competitive arena, the more they learn, even if they haven't been able to convert their knowledge into consistent success. Everything that is happening now in any competitive arena has happened before. It was in a little different form, but everything that is old is new again. These people have put in the time so that we don't have to (3.1.6 Time Limitations).

## Illustration:

These three types of people are needed in every contact network, whether we are talking about our business or our personal relationships. For our illustration, let us use the example of a person who is opening a small business. If we think that we want to open a new restaurant, what should our contact network look like?

*1. **The best source of perspective on the new competitive arena are those who have a track record of success in that arena.** When we are hired by a new employer, we need to make friends with longtime employees. When our child goes to a new school, we need to make contact with other parents more experienced in working with the school. In a new relationship, we need to make contact with people who have known the person we are dating longer than we have.

**2. *The next best source of perspective on the new competitive arena are those who know a lot of other people in an area*.** In business, trade associations and trade shows are a great place to meet old pros and develop these relationships. People who are in the business of communicating, such as salespeople and PR people, are exceptionally good local guides. They also have an incentive to develop a relationship with us because communication is their business.

**3. *The next best source of perspective on the new competitive arena are those who have a long tenure*.** It can be easy to find old pros who can act as contacts because they are easy to identify. They stand out in a crowd because they are older.

## 2.4.2 Climate Perspective

Sun Tzu's four key methods on getting perspective on temporary external conditions.

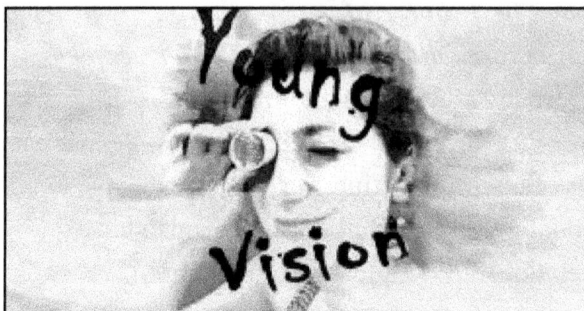

*"There are new conduits.*
*They see things differently."*

Sun Tzu's The Art of War 13:2:21-22
[Chinese Revealed Version]

*"It is the youth who sees a great opportunity hidden in just these simple services, who sees a very uncommon situation, a humble position, who gets on in the world."*
*Orison Swett Marden*

**General Principle:** Develop contacts who are in touch with what is changing.

## Situation:

As we focus on our little corner of the world, we often don't see a change coming. If changes don't fit into our historic view of what is important, we can easily miss them. The longer we are in a competitive arena ourselves, the less sensitive we are to what is changing. In today's dynamic environment, our position can degrade quickly. Our current strategic position is constantly degrading (1.1.1 Position

Dynamics). These trends can help or hinder us. We don't know from which direction they will come. Change propagates itself like a wave. The changes of climate ripple back and forth, from one end of the world to the other, affecting one competitive arena after another. As this wave of change moves through different competitive arenas, it changes its form and shape but it keeps moving, affecting us all eventually.

## Opportunity:

We want to see these changes coming from the greatest distance possible. Change is what creates our opportunities (3.2 Opportunity Creation). Our contact network gives us a broader perspective of time as well as place. Our opportunities lie not in the past or even the present but in the future (2.4.1 Ground Perspective). To get the right perspective on change, our opportunity is to see our competitive arena with fresh eyes. The faster we can learn about shifts in climate that affect us, the more of an advantage we have over others and the better positioned we are to deal with those changes.

## Key Methods:

To keep in contact with what is changing in our local neighborhood, we need to develop special channels of information that focus on change. The people most interested in change are those with the least invested in the past.

*1. Contacts who give us perspective on climate see changing trends earlier than others.* The more advance notice we have of change, the more time we have to adapt to it. This is especially true of business people, who become more focused on control and planning instead of adapting to change. This is why so many young people see the business world as boring. Most businesspeople are focused myopically on the work at hand and the current process. They are more worried about the problems that happened yesterday than the opportunities that will open tomorrow (1.8.3 Cycle Time).

**2. We need the fresh eyes of young people to provide a valuable perspective on climate change.** Hot trends sweep through the culture. Young people are the best possible source for a fresh perspective on what is new and exciting. As we get older, we are not plugged into the hot trends. Young people devote a great deal of time to what is new because they have the time to invest. They also spend more time than most communicating with their peers. The emotions and energy of the young drives the biggest changes affecting opportunity (1.4.1 Climate Shift).

**3. We must reverse our perspective to see the climate from the perspective of the young.** Young people see the changes in climate to get a fresh perspective. We have to match this perspective to understand it. To be open to what is happening in the world, we have to have an open mind. As we get older, we develop our own perspective, responsibilities, and a point of view. After a wealth of experience, we tend to take change for granted, getting less excited about it. We filter information through a wealth of mental models. We have to work directly against this tendency (3.2.5 Dynamic Reversal).

**4. We must have regular contact with young people to get a good perspective on climate.** This contact adds an invaluable perspective to our contact networks. Throughout our lives we need to develop the habit of reaching out to the latest generation and developing relationships with them. This isn't necessarily easy because communication with young people isn't necessarily easy, but it is worth the effort. The process starts with communicating an idea that they haven't heard before, that we are interested in what they think (2.2.1 Personal Relationships).

## Illustration:

The new world of computers and electronics provides some of the best illustration of these principles.

**1. Contacts who give us perspective on climate see changing trends earlier than others.** Catching a new communication trend is like catching a wave. If we don't start moving when the trend is first spotted, we can never get moving fast enough to get in sync with it and it just passes us by as the Internet passed by traditional newspapers.

*2. We need the fresh eyes of young people to provide a valuable perspective on climate change.* Many changes and trends are short-lived, but each new innovation in electronic communication, from Facebook to Twitter, that is changing the shape of our world caught on with young people first.

*3. We must reverse our perspective to see the climate from the perspective of the young.* IBM knew what other computer companies were doing, but Microsoft wasn't a computer company and it completely changed computers. The iPod did not start in the recording industry but it completely reshaped it. Starbucks did not arise from the coffee shop industry but it redefined what a cafe is.

4. *We must have regular contact with young people to get a good perspective on climate.* Some of us are fortunate to have young people in our family. Parents of young people, if they pay attention, tend to be better in touch with the latest trends. If there is a secret to including young people in our communication networks, it is not to tune them out. As our children grow up, we need new points of contact with the evolving culture. We need to reach out to young people who are relatives or belong to the same community groups that we do.

## 2.4.3 Command Perspective

Sun Tzu's six key methods for understanding developing sources for understanding decision-makers.

*"You must first know the guarding general. You must know his left and right flanks.*
*You must know his hierarchy."*
Sun Tzu's The Art of War 13:4:4-6

*"The key is to get to know people and trust them to be who they are. Instead, we trust people to be who we want them to be- and when they're not, we cry."*
*David Duchovny*

**General Principle:**  Develop information channels about key decision-makers.

## Situation:

Our success depends on the decisions of others. Their decisions depend on their unique motivations and character. Despite that, most of us invest too little on getting perspective on other people. We see their motivations and character myopically, from the point of view of our position and our friends positions. Some are so close to us that we lose our perspective. Others are so distant and anonymous that we think knowing them is impossible.

## Opportunity:

We can get better information from key aspects of character and motivation by developing the right connections (2.2.1 Personal Relationships). As we get to know decision-makers or those close to them on a personal level, we get more insight into their needs, concerns, strengths, and shortcomings. The more we know, the better we can predict the future (2.3.2 Reaction Unpredictability). The more often our actions will get the response that we want (2.3.1 Action and Reaction). The better our information channels, the better our perspective and the better our decisions.

## Key Methods:

We get to know decision makers from four different types of contacts.

*1. Our primary source of command perspective is our direct personal relationships with decision-makers:* When possible, we want to develop personal relationships with these decision makers who affect our position. This isn't always possible because some decision-makers, say our bosses, prefer to keep a distance, but often it is our shyness rather than the reticence of the decision makers that is the real problem (2.2.1 Personal Relationships).

*2. Our secondary source of command perspective are "insiders" who see different aspects of decision-makers*. People have many sides and show their different sides to different people. We see one side, others see another side. Having a range of contacts as friends helps us understand that all people are different, with different strengths, weaknesses, and challenges. If we want to get to know someone well, we are best served by developing relationships with others who know them (2.3 Personal Interactions).

*3. We get a different aspect of command perspective from those who have regular subordinate contact with decision-makers.* One of the best techniques to get information on powerful decisionmakers is to find the "low people in high places" who come in regular contact with them. Sometimes we can get close to their secretaries and assistants, but even these direct channels can be guarded. However, there are usually a host of others, office workers and services providers (trainers, barbers, etc.) who can provide valuable insights about these people's concerns and character.

*4. Historical perspective on the past actions of those in command has some limited value*. Actions speak louder than words. Historical information is valuable because people will tend to do what they have done in the past. However, our true concern is the future. Character doesn't change often, but motivations do (2.3.3 Range of Reactions , 1.6.3 Shifting Priorities).

*5. Public information is the least reliable source of perspective on those in command.* While we cannot overlook it, we have to suspect what we learn from public sources. Most public information, including rumors, should be verified before we put too much faith in them (2.1.3 Strategic Deception).

*6. Developing contacts that give us perspective on decisions-makers are the most delicate of all networking.* When getting to know someone, we collect evidence about their character, especially the five key aspects of character that relate to decision-making (1.5.1 Command Leadership).  Of course, the most powerful weapon in gathering information is simply to ask questions (2.3.4 Using Questions). If these questions are based on a sincere interest in getting to know others, they will make us friends.

# Illustration:

Let us look at two different business cases to illustrate the range of issues here: bosses and customers. We know our bosses but often have bad information on them. We too often judge them on their position rather than on their character and motivations.

*1. Our primary source of command perspective is our direct personal relationships with decision-makers.* People are often too shy to befriend their bosses or their boss's boss on a personal level. But people are people and we can find common ground with most people if we work at it to provide the basis of a relationship. Common interests, backgrounds, and histories from outside work are the best.

*2. Our secondary source of command perspective are "insiders" who see different aspects of decision-makers*. If we want to get to know our boss, for example, our fellow employees probably see pretty much the same side we do. However, another manager in a different department will know that individual in a very different way.

*3. We get a different aspect of command perspective from those who have regular subordinate contact with decision-makers.* Our bosses have secretaries, assistants, and other services providers with whom we can make a connection because we share a common contact: the boss him or herself.

*4. Historical perspective on the past actions of those in command has some limited value*. The more we can learn about our boss's own career, the more we can understand his or her character and motivation.

*5. Public information is the least reliable source of perspective on those in command.* Think of public information about the boss as a starting point for building the above types of relationships.

*6. Developing contacts that give us perspective on decisions-makers are the most delicate of all networking.* Getting information about a boss is extremely valuable, but we cannot let our boss know that we are making a project of researching him or her.

Everyone talks about knowing their customers. Unfortunately, most small businesses don't invest much in knowing their customers at all. Big businesses too delegate the task of "knowing the customer" to the "specialists" in marketing, who abstract customer motivations and care more about demographics than character.

*1. Our primary source of command perspective is our direct personal relationships with decision-makers.* Everyone who makes decisions in a business no matter what the size, should invest time in building personal relationships with some of their customers.

*2. Our secondary source of command perspective are "insiders" who see different aspects of decision-makers.* This means getting to know customers from the perspective of others who are close to them: friends and family. This is much more difficult.

*3. We get a different aspect of command perspective from those who have regular subordinate contact with decision-makers.* Where else do our customers do business? Who are their favorite service providers? We should talk to them.

*4. Historical perspective on the past actions of those in command has some limited value.* Sales histories are useful but only if we study them and their trends.

*5. Public information is the least reliable source of perspective on those in command.* Generic information about customers in the media is often too distant from our own competitive neighborhood to be valuable, but information affecting the local economy, such as plant closings, is always valuable for understanding changing motivations.

*6. Developing contacts that give us perspective on decisions-makers are the most delicate of all networking.* Customers don't like the idea that their suppliers are collecting data about their purchasing habits even when suppliers can service them better with that data.

# 2.4.4 Methods Perspective

Sun Tzu's five key methods for developing contacts who understand best practices.

*"They remain ignorant of the enemy's condition. The result is cruel."*
Sun Tzu's The Art of War 13:1:13-14

*"Fools learn from experience. I prefer to learn from the experience of others."*
*Otto von Bismarck*

**General Principle:** Learn best practices, especially from those who use systems, ideally those of our rivals.

## Situation:

When learning the best practices in our competitive arena, trial and error is the slowest possible method of discovering what works. How-to books, like our own Playbook, can give step-by-step descriptions and examples, but they are limited. The best sources about best practices are those who have been successful in a given competitive arena. We may think of those people as our competitors, but that is the wrong mindset. Most people shy away from learning their competitors' methods out of a misplaced sense of competition.

## Opportunity:

The world is filled with people who have practical experience in specific areas of skill. Many are willing to share their knowledge. The most important are those we might normally see as our competitors (1.3.1 Competitive Comparison). Strategy starts by mastering the best practices in any given competitive arena (7.2.1 Proven Methods). Those standards provide the basis for our strategic thinking. You wouldn't be reading this article unless you were interested in developing new skills in the system of strategy based upon the history of others success. The best way to learn new skills is to develop relationships with people who already have those or know the systems that we want to learn (1.5.2. Group Methods).

## Key Methods:

The following five key methods describe how we get a better perspective on best practices.

1. ***To get a perspective on best methods, we must to seek out and listen to people who have the skills and use the systems that are successful.*** Our information comes through a contact network of a limited size. Part of the network must be reserved for those who understand the "best practices" in our competitive arena. Learning proven practices allows us to find opportunities to innovate. This is

a critical path to improving our position (7.1.3 Standards and Innovation).

**2. To get a perspective on best methods, we need personal relationships with our "competitors."** When we know our competitors as people on a personal level, we see them differently. We see that they aren't our enemies. We have more in common with our rivals than anyone else. They have more to teach us in terms of methods than anyone else. Competitors aren't known for being honest with one another, nor should they be, but everything we get to know about them helps us better understand our position (1.3.1 Competitive Comparison).

**3. To get a perspective on best methods, we need to have contacts with whom our competitors work.** These are people in touch with our competition and work with or even for them. These people can give us valuable insight in how our competition works. Of course that won't endear us to our competitors if we hire away their employees, but they are a terrific source of best practices and inside information about their character (2.4.3 Command Perspective).

**4. To get a perspective on best methods, we must learn complex systems from those using them daily.** If we need to understand a system, especially complex electronic, information or mechanical systems, it is best to learn from someone who has a skill and uses the system regularly on a nuts and bolts level. This category often includes people who sell systems of various types and are familiar with a wide variety of applications. People who understand the inner workings of systems can get a lot done with very little effort (1.5.2. Group Methods).

**5. To get a perspective on best methods, our relationships based on methods must be serious.** These relationships cannot be a simply a research project. When people actually become our friends, they care about our mission. They think about their systems from the perspective of our unique needs. Harnessing the intangible capital of the human mind requires a real connection (2.2.1 Personal Relationships).

# Illustration:

We can illustrate with general observations about business that lead to very specific examples.

1. ***To get a perspective on best methods, we must to seek out and listen to people who have the skills and use the systems that are successful.*** We do not accidentally encounter the people we need to meet who know the methods that are behind success. We see successful organization, such as WalMart, but we must work to find out what systems, such as logistical systems, that are behind their success. We don't need to know the geniuses that created those systems, all we need to do is find people who know who those system work by using them When we do meet these people, we must be interested in them and listen to what they have to say.

2. ***To get a perspective on best methods, we need personal relationships with our "competitors."*** All business associations are groups of people who are potentially competitors. Associations are popular because no matter how competitive we are, we can learn from each other. Competition is not conflict. It is comparison.

3. ***To get a perspective on best methods, we need to have contacts with whom our competitors work.*** Many businesses naturally share common suppliers. Getting information about how our competitors work from these people often takes no more effort than simply asking.

4. ***To get a perspective on best methods, we must learn complex systems from those using them daily.*** Operators who do the actual work are often overlooked and undervalued within organizations. We can gain a lot simply by respecting the role they play.

5. ***To get a perspective on best methods, our relationships based on methods must be serious.*** As business people, we can get so focused on our own organizations that we don't have time to develop relationships outside of them. This is a mistake. Only those external relationships can give us perspective. At the Institute, we teach proven systems, but the principles of strategy are very general

at the Institute level. Many of our trainers take this knowledge down to the practical nuts and bolts level, applying it to specific problems in the real world. For example, Fred Leland draws upon a wealth of law enforcement and security experience working as a police officer in training other officers in strategic decision-making. The reason that we license our material to trainers like Fred is because their specific experience is as valuable as the general knowledge itself.

# 2.4.5 Mission Perspective

Sun Tzu's seven key methods on how we develop and use a perspective on motivation.

*"Place people as a single unit where they can all see and hear. You must unite them as one."*
Sun Tzu's The Art of War 7:4:7-8

*"Sprinkled in every walk of life...are a handful of people with an extraordinary knack of making friends and acquaintances."*
*Malcolm Gladwell*

**General Principle:** We focus on motivations to communicate a shared mission.

## Situation:

We develop a contact network to collect the information that we need strategically, but the network does more than collect information. It also communicates it. We cannot get information without also communicating information. The value of information is 80 percent what comes in and 20 percent what goes out. In most areas, most of the value is in what we can learn. In one area, the area of goals and mission, the value is in what others learn about us. Many people try to keep their goals a secret, but the real power of goals comes from communicating them.

## Opportunity:

People have to know our goals before they can help us (1.6 Mission Values). To help us, those in our contact network have to understand our goals and motivation. If we are asking questions, they want to know why. We have to communicate our mission in a way that gathers their support. Just as mission is the core of a strategic situation, it is the glue that holds together our contact network. Everyone within our contact network must find, in one way or another, a common cause with us (1.6.1 Shared Mission).

## Key Methods:

The following seven key methods describe how we get a better perspective on people's motivation.

*1. We cannot build a contact network without having a perspective on what motivates others to help us.* The first type of information that we want to gather from every type of contact is information about motivation. However, to be successful, we not only have to gather information about the motivations of others, we must communicate information about our motivation as well (1.6.2 Types of Motivations).

*2. Every type of contact can help us more if they understand our perspective on mission.* Those who give us perspective on the ground can help us understand the rewards within a given competitive arena (2.4.1 Ground Perspective). Those who give us perspective on the climate can help us see our opportunities (2.4.2 Climate Perspective). Those who give us perspective on the decision makers can help us see what we have in common with others (2.4.3 Command Perspective). Those who give us perspective on the methods can help us understand the benefits of certain skills and systems (2.4.4 Methods Perspective).

**3. *Our perspective on motivation allows us to create shared mission*s.** One form of opportunity is aligning people's motivations so they can work together. Incompatible motivations create conflicts, but different motivations can be aligned so everyone gets what they want (1.6.1 Shared Mission). This is the first step in identifying more specific forms of opportunities (3.0 Identifying Opportunities).

**4. *Our perspective on motivation allows us to make the shared mission exciting.*** People need stimulation and novelty. We tie together climate shifts, reward potential, character issue, and gimmicks to make the shared mission important and engaging. The higher our level of our mission and the more uniquely it is expressed, the better this works. The economics of making money is overdone and therefore boring."Professionalism"isn't much more interesting. Where we want to affect people is on the emotional and even spiritual levels of mission (2.1.4 Surprise).

**5. *Our perspective on motivation allows us to make the shared mission personal*.** We should connect our mission to our life stories and to the life stories of others. We must tell our life story in a way that helps people identify with us. Life experience creates stronger bonds than ideology. We want to give our mission an emotional connection. We connect our joy and pain to our relationships with others. We want to make it spiritual, in the sense of human spirit and destiny that we all share (2.2.1 Personal Relationships).

**6. *Our perspective on motivation allows us to transform personal contacts into missionaries*.** When our contacts support our mission, that is, share our mission, they will actively want to help us to fulfill that mission. People are interested in us because they see themselves in us and our mission. Missionaries are those who carry our message to others. Good missionaries are often able to articulate the value of supporting our mission better than we can ourselves (2.3 Personal Interactions).

**7. Our perspective on motivation allows us to identify the natural "connectors" who make the best missionaries.** Malcolm Gladwell, in his book *The Tipping Point*, explains that some people are extraordinarily well connected to a large number of others. Gladwell calls these people "connectors." We don't need to be connectors ourselves. We just need to connect with the connectors and win them over as our missionaries. Connectors are great missionaries. What makes us interesting to connectors? The same thing that makes us interesting to anyone else, our shared philosophy, our values, and goals (1.6.1 Shared Mission).

## Illustration:

Let me make this illustration personal. Let us use this illustration to promote our Science of Strategy Institute's philosophy here.

**1. We cannot build a contact network without having a perspective on what motivates others to help us.** You can use our Science of Straetgy Institute contact page (http://scienceofstrategy.org/main/contact) ask about any aspect of our system and most of the time, I will answer you personally. From your questions, we understand your motivation.

**2. Every type of contact can help us more if they understand our perspective on mission.** When we were much smaller, we would send personal emails to those who download our free Ebook *Art of War* and ask them about their motivations. Unfortunately, we seldom have time any more to do that.

**3. Our perspective on motivation allows us to create shared mission.** When we get the opportunities to visit our corporate customers to make live presentations, we always discuss how their organization's mission joins with ours in terms of helping people adapt to change.

**4. Our perspective on motivation allows us to make the shared mission exciting.** In recent years, we have increasingly focused on teaching Sun Tzu's concepts in our live presentation through activites and exercises rather than lecture. It is much more exciting for people to feel how these ideas work rather than simply hearing about them. We recognize the difference between doers and observers.

**5. *Our perspective on motivation allows us to make the shared mission personal***. In my books, on the SOSI site, and occasionally in live presentations, I illustrate Sun Tzu's ideas using my battle with cancer. It was that battle that made me refocus my life on teaching strategy to regular people. Before, I just flew around the world working with large corporations. Of course, I still do, but that isn't why I write books or created the Institute.

**6. *Our perspective on motivation allows us to transform personal contacts into missionaries***. We are support all those interesting in promoting Sun Tzu's ideas by offering them free memberships, materials, and other forms of support.

**7. *Our perspective on motivation allows us to identify the natural "connectors"who make the best missionaries***. If you are one, contact me and let's talk about what we can do together.

# 2.5 The Big Picture

Sun Tzu's nine key methods on building big picture strategic awareness.

*"If you can't see the small subtleties, you won't get the truth from spies. Pay attention to small, trifling details!"*
Sun Tzu's The Art of War 13:3:7-8

*"Each time we do a successful operation it allows us to slap new pieces of the puzzle in. We get a clearer picture. We're able to get more information."*
*Steve Russell*

**General Principle:** Put together the strategic puzzle by building on the model framework.

## Situation:

Developing strategic perspective is like putting together the pieces of a puzzle. We are exposed to a flood of information. Each piece of information seems disconnected. When we cannot fit information into a larger picture, it is quickly lost and forgotten. Everyone is trying to build up a picture of their strategic position. Most of these pictures lack a framework to give them structure. Information is loosely and randomly connected. The resulting picture is both sketchy and fragile. Without a framework, understanding is limited. Disconnected pieces of information are lost.

## Opportunity:

Our minds recognize and remember patterns. We can see patterns even when we look at the random dots. Our ancestors looked at the stars in the sky and saw pictures. This is the way our minds work. The mental models of Sun Tzu leverage the way our minds work. His mental models were developed and preserved down the centuries because they work. Our opportunity is in making them work for us. They provide the framework around which we build our strategic perspective. With this foundation, we can manage more information. With this framework, we can quickly separate the relevant from the irrelevant. We can verify information because it is consistent with the framework (2.2.2 Mental Models).

## Key Methods:

The following nine key methods describe how we put details into a larger, more comprehensive picture.

*1. Sun Tzu's mental models are the framework, the scaffolding for creating a big picture perspective*. To make them relevant to our specific situation, we have to flesh out that framework. We must fill these models with information from our unique situation, putting together the little pieces of information into a more comprehensive and powerful picture (2.2.2 Mental Models).

**2. Big picture perspective requires a flow of information from a contact network.** News is not information. We develop contact networks specifically to get the types of information most relevant to our situation (2.4 Contact Networks).

**3. Big picture perspective sorts detailed information using the mental model of the five elements.** This model gives us a structure for organizing what we learn. While we cannot remember a lot of separate details, we remember connected details. No detail is too small when it comes to putting together a puzzle. A piece of information that seems trivial by itself can be telling once we try to fit it into a larger picture. This picture allows us to understand our basic position, how it is changing, and how it is likely to change in the future.   (1.3 Elemental Analysis).

**4. Big picture perspective highlights the most relevant information as keys to advancing our position.** This information is the most relevant because we can act on it. These models include identifying hidden opportunities, picking high-probabilities opportunities, responding to common situations, and so on (1.8 Progress Cycle).

**5. As we flesh out our big picture perspective, it becomes easier to fit in new pieces and identify mission pieces.** Going back to our puzzle analogy, each piece of information that we put in place makes it easier and faster to put new pieces into place. The blank areas in the puzzle also indicate where we must look for needed information. We learn the mental models of Sun Tzu's strategy to help us quickly sort the information that comes in so that it doesn't pile up but those models are more powerful as we flesh them out. The character of each piece can be identified quickly and put in a place where it provides us the most insight. (2.1 Information Value).

**6. Information that doesn't fit into our big picture perspective draws our attention.** As we put together our picture of the situation, the pieces have to fit. Pieces that don't fit tell us something important. Some pieces won't fit because they aren't right. If many pieces don't fit, they challenge our assumptions about how we are putting together the puzzle. A tiny piece of information can turn out to be the key in fitting everything together in a way that makes better sense. We know that much of our information is subjective and therefore prone to error.It is only by fitting the pieces of information together that we see how one piece of information confirms another (2.1.1 Information Limits).

**7. *Our decisions must be based on our big picture perspective, not separate events or elements*.** We can trust any specific data point at our own risk. We instead trust the picture. It is not the independent pieces that matter, but how they all fit together. None of the pieces of an airplane have the ability to fly, but when they are put together, that capability emerges. Knowing how to put the pieces together is the difference between a confusing series of events that pull us first in one direction and then another and having a map of the terrain (5.1.1 Event Pressure).

**8. *Our big picture perspective is more valuable when it joins our picture with those of others*.** When we work with other people using the same mental models, we amplify our abilities. We help them and they help us create our perspective of the strategic situation. Given common models and a common language, our pictures can quickly be connected with those of others to deepen and broaden our insight (2.2.3 Standard Terminology).

**9. *The process of building our big picture perspective never stops*.** We continue building and refining our picture of our situation throughout our lives. As some parts are outdated, new parts replace them but, correctly built, the picture grows more and more detailed and dependable over time (1.8.2 The Adaptive Loop).

## Illustration:

Let us apply to these principles to the task of finding a better job.

**1. *Sun Tzu's mental models are the framework, the scaffolding for creating a big picture perspective*.** In searching for a job, most people are like pin balls, bouncing around randomly until they fall into a hole. Using the methods above in my personal career when I was in the job market, I managed to advance my position on the average of every eight months.

**2. Big picture perspective requires a flow of information from a contact network.** Starting with our current contacts, we should grow the network in the direction of where we want to go based on what we have done in the past.

**3. Big picture perspective sorts detailed information using the mental model of the five elements.** We begin to see our job area more completely, seeing where old opportunities are fading while others are opening up.

**4. Big picture perspective highlights the most relevant information as keys to advancing our position.** We start focusing on where opportunities are opening up, identifying where to look for the high-probability opportunities and how to best pursue them.

**5. As we flesh out our big picture perspective, it becomes easier to fit in new pieces and identify mission pieces.** As we look in more and more specific areas of opportunity, we develop an even more detailed picture. This picture helps us compare alternatives to see which hold the greatest opportunity for us personally.

**6. Information that doesn't fit into our big picture perspective draws our attention.** Rejection is information. Our ideas about what job we should be looking for changes as we realize that many of the opportunities we were pursuing have a very low-probability of success.

**7. Our decisions must be based on our big picture perspective not separate events or elements.** When we go to interviews, it is because we understand the job market and how we fit into it.

**8. Our big picture perspective is more valuable when it joins our picture with those of others.** We share our picture with our potential employers, demonstrating that we are not just looking for a job, but a career. If we demonstrate that we have a valuable perspective, we stand out dramatically from other applications.

**9. The process of building our big picture perspective never stops.** Not only does each interview improve our picture, but over our whole career, we use this process to continually advance our position.

# 2.6 Knowledge Leverage

Sun Tzu's five key methods for getting competitive value out of knowledge.

LEVERAGE

"Give me a place to stand, and I will move the Earth." - Archimedes

*"Knowledge is victory.*
*No knowledge is no victory."*
Sun Tzu's The Art of War 1:1:36-37
[Chinese Revealed version]

*"As a small businessperson, you have no greater*
*leverage than the truth."*

*Paul Keating*

**General Principle:** Knowledge must get more value out of our resources.

## Situation:

Despite the progress demonstrated by human history, there is a strong school of thought that claims that success is a zero-sum game. To advance our position, we must take from others. For those who see life as a zero-sum game, growth and progress can only end badly. It suggests that as the world grows and advances, we must all grow poorer because our limited resources are split among more and more people. Populations must therefore be controlled. People must be stopped from building and consuming because everything requires resources. From this perspective, the only moral strategy is to give up on personal progress and success.

## Opportunity:

Sun Tzu's perspective on making choices maintains that real, lasting progress can be made, not only for the few but for all. He sees the only real resource as the human mind. The value of all other resources come from our knowledge of how to use those resources. The human mind can continually create more value out of once useless resources through learning. The only limited resources are our knowledge, our freedom to make decisions, and our capacity for understanding. More minds means more knowledge, freedom, and capacity, which means we get more value out of existing resources. This understanding turns our fears inside out. Population growth creates more minds that can create more value. Hong Kong and Singapore are rich despite their lack of resources. More progress creates less costly forms of value improving our environment. Our opportunity is to enrich the world by getting more value from undervalued resources, starting with our own time (7.6 Non-Zero Sum Games).

## Key Methods:

The following five key methods describe Sun Tzu's perspective on the creation of value from knowledge.

1. ***Knowledge leverage means combining information with proven mental models to create value.*** Information alone is not knowledge. We must use this information to create knowledge and produce value. The old saying is that it takes money to make money.

The real truth is it takes knowledge to make money or, more pre-cisely, to make progress. Money, like all resources, is wasted if it is not put into a model that works (2.5 The Big Picture).

**2. *Our success depends directly on our ability to leverage knowledge.*** Sun Tzu's system is built on getting rewards from making investments. Profit measures the value of our knowledge exactly. It is the difference between the value we purchase and the value that we generate. Profit depends on our knowledge. We must know what to buy, how and where to buy it, what to make, and how and where to sell it (3.1.2 Strategic Profitability).

**3. *Information leverage requires an investment.*** Though knowledge can replace every other cost, learning also has its costs. It must never be taken for granted. It requires time and effort to create and maintain the type of contact networks defined by Sun Tzu's strategy, but the costs of maintaining an information network goes beyond time and effort alone (2.2 Information Gathering).

**4. *Leverage knowledge value by replacing other forms more costly resources.*** The right knowledge saves time, materials, and effort. Good knowledge leverages available resources by allow-ing us to put those resources at the right place at the right time. The better our knowledge, the better our decisions about what to buy, where to buy it, what to produce, and how to produce it. This decision-making is the difference between success and failure (2.1 Information Value).

**5. *When people who provide us with valuable information the we can leverage, we must share the rewards.*** We must actively provide our contacts an incentive to think about us. When they hear information that might be valuable, we want them to think to pass it on. Knowledge is so valuable that no reward is too generous for those who can give us the right information at the right time. These rewards reinforce the relationship and communicate what we see as valuable. Rewards can be as simple as showing honest interest in the lives of our contacts. One of the best rewards is to pass on valu-able information to them (2.3 Personal Interactions).

# Illustration:

Let us look at the knowledge of competitive strategy, specifically at the knowledge that Sun Tzu teaches from this perspective.

*1. Knowledge leverage means combining information with proven mental models to create value.* We get a flow of competitive information from the environment, Sun Tzu's key methods give us proven mental models to convert that information into advances in our position.

*2. Our success depends directly on our ability to leverage knowledge.* Our success in competition depends on our knowledge of what competition really is and how it works. Being successful in external competition is simply a matter of knowing the principles of Sun Tzu better than those with whom we are competing.

*3. Information leverage requires an investment.* The most expensive way to learn competitive strategy is through trial and error. The materials and classes that the Institute offers are inexpensive in comparison, but they still require you to spend time in study and practice.

*4. Leverage knowledge value by replacing other forms more costly resources.* The real price that we pay for not learning competitive strategy is in the cost of lost opportunities. By not seeing our opportunities and not knowing how to take advantage of them, we pay a price in terms of our success in life.

*5. When people who provide us with valuable information the we can leverage, we must share the rewards.* If people didn't reward the Institute by purchasing our publications and training, we couldn't afford to provide this information. Because we can provide this value, more and more people are successful all over the world and we, in turn, are rewarded for the part we play in helping create that success.

# 2.7 Information Secrecy

Sun Tzu's nine key methods defining the role of secrecy in relationships.

*"No work is as secret as that of spies."*
Sun Tzu's The Art of War 13:3:5

*"If knowledge is power, clandestine knowledge is power squared; it can be withheld, exchanged, and leveraged."*
*Letty Cottin*

**General Principle:** We must know where secrecy is required to maintain our flow of valuable information.

## Situation:

We can undermine our position by sharing the wrong information with the wrong people. People are not born with an inherent understanding of the principles of secrecy. These principles arise because knowledge is power. We must always consider how the power of our knowledge can be used against us. Knowledge about what we know or don't know is power over us. The challenge is that our ability to leverage knowledge depends on other people. We must give information in order to get information. People cannot support us unless they know us. We must therefore walk a tight rope, a dangerous balance of keeping information secret while sharing information.

## Opportunity:

We all use secrecy to deny our rivals good information about our positions and direction. Skilled use of secrecy actually improves our ability to get information. It is critical in maintaining contact networks because our friends expect us to keep their confidential information secret. Our opportunity is in understanding when information is most valuable in public and when it is most valuable in secret. We do not have to publicize information in order to use it. We do not have to reveal what we know in making a move. This means understanding the different levels of relationships, the privacy expectations of each level, and the consequences of privacy being violated.

## Key Methods:

There are nine key methods describing three different types of relationships and their requirements for secrecy.

*1. We should keep all information secret unless we get leverage from publicizing it and then we must protect our sources.*
Our default position should be secrecy. We give away information when we talk and when we act. We cannot leverage our knowledge

without communicating it. However, leveraging information is not as important as assuring that we continue to get new information. We must balance these two needs using the key methods below (2.6 Knowledge Leverage).

**2. The principles of secrecy operate differently on personal relationships, authority relationships, and social relationships.** One-to-one relationships are *personal connections,* where communication is the more free and the highest level of trust comes into play. One-to-many relationships are *authority connections,* where information flows are more filtered and controlled and the next highest level of privacy is expected. Many-to-many relationships are *social connections,* that provide us with the most general information and have the least expectation of privacy. These three areas can overlap. A social relationship can have a small element of personal connection. A authority relationship can have an element of social connection. These relationships are different because the motivations around which they are formed are different (1.6.2 Types of Motivations).

**3. Secrecy is important because violating privacy expectations degrades higher levels of relationships.** Each of us is constrained by the privacy expectations of others and they are constrained by us. A violation of those constraints always degrades the relationship, decreasing its importance. People leave personal and authority relationships based on these violations. When sensitive information from a one-to-one relationship is shared, what was once a personal relationship, entitled to private information, becomes an authority or social relationship. Serious violations destroy relationships and potentially creates enemies (7.2.2 Preparing Expectations).

**4. Sensitive or secret information is a matter of personal opinion.** All relationships include a variety of facts and opinions, but privacy expectations only extend to sensitive information. Unfortunately, what others consider sensitive is not always obvious. We must be very clear about what we consider sensitive information without expecting others to ask. On the other hand, we must ask to know what others consider sensitive without expecting them to be clear. Everyone has their own rules (2.3.4 Using Questions).

**5. *Key one-to-one relationships also have the highest expectations of secrecy and privacy.*** These relationships are the most costly to maintain, but they are also the most critical to our success. We want to be able to share very private perspectives with others in our network and we hope that they will share their most private perspectives with us. The ability to keep confidences is a cornerstone of contact networks. Information from personal relationships, where the most confidential information is shared, cannot cross over into social or authority relationships where information is the less sensitive. If people within our contact network violate our confidences, we can no longer share confidential information with them (2.3 Personal Interactions).

**6. *Authority relationships have more complex expectations of secrecy and privacy.*** Information from these relationships can be shared with our personal relationships but not in our social ones. Within the hierarchy, authority-based information can always be shared up (but information from personal relationships cannot). However, authority information can only be shared down with direction from above (1.5.1 Command Leadership).

**7. *When sharing information, the principles of secrecy depend on the other person's view of our relationship.*** People do not judge us based upon our view of the relationship, but their own. We must be sensitive to their perceptions because relationships are subjective. We make mistakes when we act from our viewpoint rather than considering the subjective viewpoints of others (1.2 Subobjective Positions).

**8. *The principles of secrecy are most likely to be violated when relationships change.*** Relationships at every level not stable nor are they exclusive. People can move up and down among these three levels and within a given level. Even one-to-one relationships can rise and fall in importance. If a member of our contact network develops a closer relationship with one of our rivals, we must expect our confidences to be shared (1.1.1 Position Dynamics).

**9. *We must continually adapt our judgments about sharing information and secrecy.*** Both information and misinformation is shared within contact networks. Sharing information tends to strengthen relationships while misinformation tends to weaken them. In situations where relationships change and we are fortunate enough to learn about it, we have an opportunity to use the contact as a channel for misleading information or disinformation (2.1.3 Strategic Deception).

## Illustration:

Let us illustrate how these principles work within romantic relationships because they offer the funniest examples.

**1. *We should keep all information secret unless we get leverage from publicizing it and then we must protect our sources.*** An engagement or marriage is a public announcement because it benefits both parties and society to publicize it. However, most of what happens between a couple is kept secret or should be.

**2. *The principles of secrecy operate differently on personal relationships, authority relationships, and social relationships.*** By romantic relationships we mean personal relationships.

**3. *Secrecy is important because violating privacy expectations degrades higher levels of relationships.*** If your romantic significant other tells you a secret, telling it to your best friend has painful consequences.

**4. *Sensitive or secret information is a matter of personal opinion.*** Sorry, you won't get out of it by telling someone you didn't know that the information was sensitive. If you didn't ask, you're an idiot for not knowing.

**5. *Key one-to-one relationships also have the highest expectations of secrecy and privacy.*** If your spouse tells you something sensitive, you do not share it with your boss.

**6. *Authority relationships have more complex expectations of secrecy and privacy.*** You must tell your spouse what your boss told you to keep a secret. There is authority and higher authority.

**7. *When sharing information, the principles of secrecy depend on the other person's view of our relationship.*** We may think the relationship is personal but the other person may think it is merely social and therefore free to tell whatever we confide in them to other friends.

**8. *The principles of secrecy are most likely to be violated when relationships change.*** When you break up a romantic relationship, expect those pictures to appear on the Internet.

**9. *We must continually adapt our judgments about sharing information and secrecy.*** If you think a relationship is in trouble, you might want to be a little bit careful about what you share.

# Glossary of Key Concepts from
## Sun Tzu's *The Art of War*

This glossary is keyed to the most common English words used in the translation of *The Art of War*. Those terms only capture the strategic concepts generally. Though translated as English nouns, verbs, adverbs, or adjectives, the Chinese characters on which they are based are totally conceptual, not parts of speech. For example, the character for conflict is translated as the noun "conflict," as the verb "fight," and as the adjective "disputed." Ancient written Chinese was a conceptual language, not a spoken one. More like mathematical terms, these concepts are primarily defined by the strict structure of their relationships with other concepts. The Chinese names shown in parentheses with the characters are primarily based on Pinyin, but we occasionally use Cantonese terms to make each term unique.

**Advance** (*Jeun* 進): to move into new **ground**; to expand your **position**; to move forward in a campaign; the opposite of **flee**.

**Advantage, *benefit*** (*Li* 利)**:** an opportunity arising from having a better **position** relative to an **enemy**; an opening left by an **enemy**; a **strength** that matches against an **enemy's weakness**; where fullness meets emptiness; a desirable characteristic of a strategic **position**.

**Aim, *vision, foresee*** (*Jian* 見)**: focus** on a specific **advantage**, opening, or opportunity; predicting movements of an **enemy**; a skill of a **leader** in observing **climate**.

**Analysis, *plan*** (*Gai* 計): a comparison of relative **position**; the examination of the five factors that define a strategic **position**; a combination of **knowledge** and **vision**; the ability to see through **deception**.

**Army:** see **war**.

**Attack, *invade*** (*Gong* 攻): a movement to new **ground**; advancing a strategic **position**; action against an **enemy** in the sense of moving into his **ground**; opposite of **defend**; does not necessarily mean **conflict**.

**Bad, *ruined*** (*Pi* 圮): a condition of the **ground** that makes **advance** difficult; destroyed; terrain that is broken and difficult to traverse; one of the nine situations or types of terrain.

**Barricaded:** see **obstacles**.

**Battle** (*Zhan* 戰): to challenge; to engage an **enemy**; generically, to meet a challenge; to choose a confrontation with an **enemy** at a specific time and place; to focus all your resources on a task; to establish superiority in a **position**; to challenge an **enemy** to increase **chaos**; that which is **controlled** by **surprise**; one of the four forms of **attack**; the response to a **desperate situation**; character meaning was originally "big meeting," though later took on the meaning "big weapon"; not necessarily **conflict**.

**Bravery, *courage*** (<u>Yong</u> 勇): the ability to face difficult choices; the character quality that deals with the changes of **CLIMATE;** courage of conviction; willingness to act on vision; one of the six characteristics of a leader.

**Break, *broken*, *divided*** (<u>Po</u> 破): to **divide** what is **complete**; the absence of a **uniting philosophy**; the opposite of <u>unity</u>.

**Calculate, *count*** (<u>Shu</u> 数): mathematical comparison of quantities and qualities; a measurement of **distance** or troop size.

**Change, *transform*** (<u>Bian</u> 變): transition from one **condition** to another; the ability to adapt to different situations; a natural characteristic of **climate**.

**Chaos, *disorder*** (<u>Juan</u> 亂): **conditions** that cannot be **foreseen**; the natural state of confusion arising from **battle**; one of six weaknesses of an organization; the opposite of **control**.

**Claim, *position*, *form*** (<u>Xing</u> 形): to use the **ground**; a shape or specific condition of **ground**; the **ground** that you **control**; to use the benefits of the **ground**; the formations of troops; one of the four key skills in making progress.

**Climate, *heaven*** (<u>Tian</u> 天): the passage of time; the realm of uncontrollable **change**; divine providence; the weather; trends that **change** over time; generally, the future; what one must **aim** at in the future; one of five key factors in **analysis**; the opposite of **ground**.

**Command** (<u>Ling</u> 令): to order or the act of ordering subordinates; the decisions of a **leader**; the creation of **methods**.

**Competition:** see <u>war</u>.

**Complete:** see <u>unity</u>.

**Condition:** see **ground**.

**Confined, *surround*** (<u>Wei</u> 圍): to encircle; a **situation** or **stage** in which your options are limited; the proper tactic for dealing with an **enemy** that is ten times smaller; to seal off a smaller **enemy**; the characteristic of a **stage** in which a larger **force** can be attacked by a smaller one; one of nine **situations** or **stages**.

**Conflict, *fight*** (<u>Zheng</u> 爭): to contend; to dispute; direct confrontation of arms with an **enemy**; highly desirable **ground** that creates disputes; one of nine types of **ground**, terrain, or stages.

**Constricted, *narrow*** (<u>Ai</u> 狹): a confined space or niche; one of six field positions; the limited extreme of the dimension distance; the opposite of **spread-out**.

**Control, *govern*** (<u>Chi</u> 治): to manage situations; to overcome disorder; the opposite of **chaos**.

**Dangerous:** see **serious**.

**Dangers, *adverse*** (Ak 阨): a condition that makes it difficult to **advance**; one of three dimensions used to evaluate advantages; the dimension with the extreme field **positions** of **entangling** and **supporting**.

**Death, *desperate*** (_Si_ 死): to end or the end of life or efforts; an extreme situation in which the only option is **battle**; one of nine **stages** or types of **terrain**; one of five types of **spies**; opposite of **survive**.

**Deception, *bluffing, illusion*** (_Gui_ 詭):
to control perceptions; to control information; to mislead an **enemy**; an attack on an opponent's **aim**; the characteristic of war that confuses perceptions.

**Defend** (_Shou_ 守): to guard or to hold a **ground**; to remain in a **position**; the opposite of **attack**.

**Detour** (_Yu_ 迂): the indirect or unsuspected path to a **position**; the more difficult path to **advantage**; the route that is not **direct**.

**Direct, *straight*** (_Jik_ 直.): a straight or obvious path to a goal; opposite of **detour**.

**Distance, *distant*** (_Yuan_ 遠): the space separating **ground**; to be remote from the current location; to occupy **positions** that are not close to one another; one of six field positions; one of the three dimensions for evaluating opportunities; the emptiness of space.

**Divide, *separate*** (_Fen_ 分): to break apart a larger force; to separate from a larger group; the opposite of **join** and **focus**.

**Double agent, *reverse*** (_Fan_ 反): to turn around in direction; to change a situation; to switch a person's allegiance; one of five types of spies.

**Easy, *light*** (_Qing_ 輕): to require little effort; a **situation** that requires little effort; one of nine **stages** or types of terrain; opposite of **serious**.

**Emotion, *feeling*** (_Xin_ 心): an unthinking reaction to **aim**, a necessary element to inspire **moves**; a component of esprit de corps; never a sufficient cause for **attack**.

**Enemy, *competitor*** (_Dik_ 敵): one who makes the same **claim**; one with a similar **goal**; one with whom comparisons of capabilities are made.

**Entangling, *hanging*** (_Gua_ 懸): a **position** that cannot be returned to; any **condition** that leaves no easy place to go; one of six field positions.

**Evade, *avoid*** (_Bi_ 避): the tactic used by small competitors when facing large opponents.

**Fall apart, *collapse*** (_Beng_ 崩): to fail to execute good decisions; to fail to use a **constricted position**; one of six weaknesses of an organization.

**Fall down, *sink*** (_Haam_ 陷): to fail to make good decisions; to **move** from a **supporting position**; one of six weaknesses of organizations.

**Feelings, *affection, love*** (_Ching_ 情): the bonds of relationship; the result of a shared **philosophy**; requires management.

**Fight, *struggle*** (Dou 鬥): to engage in **conflict**; to face difficulties.

**Fire** (_Huo_ 火): an environmental weapon; a universal analogy for all weapons.

**Flee, *retreat, northward*** (_Bei_ 北) :to abandon a **position**; to surrender ground; one of six weaknesses of an **army**; opposite of **advance**.

**Focus, *concentrate*** (_Zhuan_ 專): to bring resources together at a given time; to **unite** forces for a purpose; an attribute of having a shared **philosophy**; the opposite of *divide*.

**Force** (_Lei_ 力): power in the simplest sense; a **group** of people bound by **unity** and **focus**; the relative balance of **strength** in opposition to **weakness**.

**Foresee:** see **aim**.

**Fullness:** see **strength**.

**General:** see **leader**.

**Goal:** see **philosophy**.

**Ground, *situation, stage*** (_Di_ 地): the earth; a specific place; a specific condition; the place one competes; the prize of competition; one of five key factors in competitive analysis; the opposite of **climate**.

**Groups, *troops*** (_Dui_ 隊): a number of people united under a shared **philosophy**; human resources of an organization; one of the five targets of fire attacks.

**Inside, *internal*** (_Nei_ 內): within a **territory** or organization; an insider; one of five types of spies; opposite of _Wai_, outside.

**Intersecting, *highway*** (_Qu_ 衢): a **situation** or **ground** that allows you to **join**; one of nine types of terrain.

**Join** (_Hap_ 合): to unite; to make allies; to create a larger **force**; opposite of **divide**.

**Knowledge, *listening*** (_Zhi_: 知): to have information; the result of listening; the first step in advancing a **position**; the basis of strategy.

**Lax, *loosen*** (_Shii_ 弛): too easygoing; lacking discipline; one of six weaknesses of an army.

**Leader, *general, commander*** (_Jiang_ 將): the decision-maker in a competitive unit; one who **listens** and **aims**; one who manages **troops**; superior of officers and men; one of the five key factors in analysis; the conceptual opposite of fa, the established methods, which do not require decisions.

**Learn, *compare*** (_Xiao_ 效): to evaluate the relative qualities of **enemies**.

**Listen, *obey*** (_Ting_ 聽): to gather **knowledge**; part of **analysis**.

**Listening:** see **knowledge**.

**Local, *countryside* (*Xiang* 鄉)**: the nearby **ground**; to have **knowledge** of a specific **ground**; one of five types of **spies**.

**Marsh (*Ze* 澤)**: **ground** where footing is unstable; one of the four types of **ground**; analogy for uncertain situations.

**Method**: see **system**.

**Mission**: see **philosophy**.

**Momentum, *influence* (*Shi* 勢)**: the **force** created by **surprise** set up by **standards**; used with **timing**.

**Mountains, *hill, peak* (*Shan* 山)**: uneven **ground**; one of four types of **ground**; an analogy for all unequal **situations**.

**Move, *march, act* (*Hang* 行)**: action toward a position or goal; used as a near synonym for _dong_, act.

**Nation (*Guo* 國)**: the state; the productive part of an organization; the seat of political power; the entity that controls an **army** or competitive part of the organization.

**Obstacles, *barricaded* (*Xian* 險)**: to have barriers; one of the three characteristics of the **ground**; one of six field positions; as a field position, opposite of **unobstructed**.

**Open, *meeting, crossing* (*Jiao* 來)**: to share the same **ground** without conflict; to come together; a **situation** that encourages a race; one of nine **terrains** or **stages**.

**Opportunity**: see _advantage._

**Outmaneuver (*Sou* 走)**: to go astray; to be **forced** into a **weak position**; one of six weaknesses of an army.

**Outside, *external* (*Wai* 外)**: not within a **territory** or **army**; one who has a different perspective; one who offers an objective view; opposite of **internal**.

**Philosophy, *mission, goals* (*Tao* 道)**: the shared **goals** that **unite** an **army**; a system of thought; a shared viewpoint; literally "the way"; a way to work together; one of the five key factors in **analysis**.

**Plateau (*Liu* 陸)**: a type of **ground** without defects; an analogy for any equal, solid, and certain **situation**; the best place for competition; one of the four types of **ground**.

**Resources, *provisions* (*Liang* 糧)**: necessary supplies, most commonly food; one of the five targets of fire attacks.

**Restraint:** see **timing.**

**Reward, *treasure, money*** (*Bao* 賞): profit; wealth; the necessary compensation for competition; a necessary ingredient for **victory**; **victory** must pay.

**Scatter, *dissipating*** (*San* 散): to disperse; to lose **unity**; the pursuit of separate **goals** as opposed to a central **mission**; a situation that causes a **force** to scatter; one of nine conditions or types of terrain.

**Serious, *heavy*** (*Chong* 重): any task requiring effort and skill; a **situation** where resources are running low when you are deeply committed to a campaign or heavily invested in a project; a situation where opposition within an organization mounts; one of nine **stages** or types of **terrain.**

**Siege** (*Gong Cheng* 攻城): to move against entrenched positions; any movement against an **enemy's strength**; literally "strike city"; one of the four forms of attack; the least desirable form of attack.

**Situation:** see **ground.**

**Speed, *hurry*** (Sai 馳): to **move** over **ground** quickly; the ability to **advance positions** in a minimum of time; needed to take advantage of a window of opportunity.

**Spread-out, *wide*** (*Guang* 廣): a surplus of **distance**; one of the six **ground positions**; opposite of **constricted.**

**Spy, *conduit, go-between*** (*Gaan* 間): a source of information; a channel of communication; literally, an "opening between."

**Stage:** see **ground.**

**Standard, *proper, correct*** (*Jang* 正): the expected behavior; the standard approach; proven methods; the opposite of surprise; together with **surprise** creates **momentum.**

**Storehouse, *house*** (*Ku* 庫): a place where resources are stockpiled; one of the five targets for fire attacks.

**Stores, *accumulate, savings*** (*Ji* 糧): resources that have been stored; any type of inventory; one of the five targets of fire attacks.

**Strength, *fullness, satisfaction*** (*Sat* 壹): wealth or abundance or resources; the state of being crowded; the opposite of Xu, empty.

**Supply wagons, *transport*** (*Zi* 輜): the movement of **resources** through **distance**; one of the five targets of fire attacks.

**Support, *supporting*** (*Zhii* 支): to prop up; to enhance; a **ground position** that you cannot leave without losing **strength**; one of six field positions; the opposite extreme of gua, entangling.

**Surprise, *unusual, strange*** (*Qi* 奇) : the unexpected; the innovative; the opposite of **standard**; together with **standards** creates **momentum**.

**Surround**: see **confined**.

**Survive,** *live, birth* (*Shaang* 生): the state of being created, started, or beginning; the state of living or surviving; a temporary condition of fullness; one of five types of spies; the opposite of **death**.

**System,** *method* (*Fa* 法): a set of procedures; a group of techniques; steps to accomplish a **goal**; one of the five key factors in analysis; the realm of groups who must follow procedures; the opposite of the **leader**.

**Territory,** *terrain*: see **ground**.

**Timing,** *restraint* (*Jie* 節): to withhold action until the proper time; to release tension; a companion concept to **momentum**.

**Troops**: see **group**.

**Unity,** *whole, oneness* (*Yi* 一): the characteristic of a **group** that shares a **philosophy**; the lowest number; a **group** that acts as a unit; the opposite of **divided**.

**Unobstructed,** *expert* (*Tong* 通): without obstacles or barriers; **ground** that allows easy movement; open to new ideas; one of six field positions; opposite of **obstructed**.

**Victory,** *win, winning* (*Sing* 勝): success in an endeavor; getting a reward; serving your mission; an event that produces more than it consumes; to make a profit.

**War,** *competition, army* (**Bing** 兵): a dynamic situation in which **positions** can be won or lost; a contest in which a **reward** can be won; the conditions under which the principles of strategy work.

**Water,** *river* (*Shui* 水): a fast-changing **ground**; fluid **conditions**; one of four types of **ground**; an analogy for change.

**Weakness,** *emptiness, need* (*Xu* 虛): the absence of people or resources; devoid of **force**; the point of **attack** for an **advantage;** a characteristic of **ground** that enables **speed**; poor; the opposite of strength.

**Win,** *winning*: see **victory**.

**Wind,** *fashion, custom* (*Feng* 風): the pressure of environmental forces.

# The *Art of War Playbook* Series

There are over two-hundred and thirty articles on Sun Tzu's competitive principles in the nine volumes of the *Art of War Playbook*. Each volume covers a specific area of Sun Tzu strategy.

# About the Translator and Author

Gary Gagliardi is recognized as America's leading expert on Sun Tzu's *The Art of War*. An award-winning author and business strategist, his many books on Sun Tzu's strategy have been translated around the world. He has appeared on hundreds of talk shows nationwide, providing strategic insight on the breaking news. He has trained decision makers from some of the world's most successful organizations in competitive thinking. His workshops convert Sun Tzu's many principles into a series of practical tools for handling common competitive challenges.

Gary began using Sun Tzu's competitive principles in a successful corporate career and when he started his own software company. In 1990, he wrote his first *Art of War* adaptation for his company's salespeople. By 1992, his company was on *Inc. Magazine's* list of the 500 fastest-growing privately held companies in America. He personally won the U.S. Chamber of Commerce Blue Chip Quality Award and was an Ernst and Young Entrepreneur of the Year finalist. His customers—AT&T, GE, and Motorola, among others—began inviting him to speak at their conferences. After becoming a multimillionaire when he sold his software company in 1997, he continued teaching *The Art of War* around the world.

Gary has authored several breakthrough works on *The Art of War*. Ten of his books on strategy have won book award recognition in nine different non-fiction categories.

# Other *Art of War* Books
# by Gary Gagliardi

Gary Gagliardi's Books are Available at:
SunTzus.com
Amazon.com
BarnesAndNoble.com
Itunes.apple.com

www.ingramcontent.com/pod-product-compliance
Lightning Source LLC
Chambersburg PA
CBHW071837200326

41519CB00016B/4144